Some Other Books by Babette Deutsch

THE COLLECTED POEMS
OF
BABETTE DEUTSCH

The
Collected Poems
of
Babette Deutsch

Garden City, New York

DOUBLEDAY & COMPANY, INC.

1969

Library of Congress Catalog Card Number 68-22508

TO A CERTAIN FEW

AMONG THE LIVING AND, IF AMONG THE DEAD,

REMEMBERED LIVING

FOREWORD

The poems with which this book opens were written after those included in a previous collection published in 1963. Most of the others have been chosen from eight of my nine volumes of verse. Except for the position of the new work, the arrangement is roughly chronological. Along with more recent poems, there have been added old ones in revised versions, a few pieces of light verse, two examples of juvenilia also presumed to be entertaining, which were composed when I was five and seven years old, respectively, and some translations. Several other poems might perhaps be considered juvenilia, since they were written in my undergraduate days. As some of them were published in such periodicals as *The New Republic* and *The North American Review*, and appeared subsequently in my first book, they seem to warrant inclusion in Part II. One early poem, published in *The Dial* for September, 1921, under the title "And Again to Po Chü-I", has been so thoroughly revised as to constitute practically a new poem and has therefore been placed in Part I, under the title "To Po Chü-I". Originally "Piano Recital" was dedicated to Maro Ajemian and John Cage, but because it speaks of the traditional part of the program I have now dedicated it to the pianist alone, and dedicated to the avant-garde composer a new poem about work of his heard at the same recital. On learning that I planned a section devoted to light verse, Allen Tate urged me to include my response to the Tates' Christmas greeting for 1967. At his repeated instance, I offer it here with his lines. As these pages go to press, I note sadly that Michael has died.

> Where there were two there now are four
> To light the yule unlatch the door
> for those dear friends we wish were here

[ix]

to raise a glass of Christmas cheer
for Michael Pollux and Castor John
on whom the Lord has smiled and shone
and on you too we pray He'll smile
as all our four send love meanwhile

1967   *Helen and Allen Tate*
                              John and Michael

Dear Helen, Allen, Michael, John,
You give us joys to think upon:
The world's more radiant, thanks to you.
May it, then, be so for you, too.
May you enjoy such holiday
Pleasures as come your fourfold way.
Yes, and may 1968
Find you, and leave you, most elate.
These wishes, strong, affectionate,
Are from Avrahm and from Babette.

Among the omitted pieces is one that received an award,
several that have been anthologized, a sonnet sequence presented as the Phi Beta Kappa poem at Columbia University
in 1929, and the book-length poem, *Epistle to Prometheus*.
None of these is now acceptable to me, and I have been
unable to rework any of them to my satisfaction. I have
also omitted translations that I believe to be equal to those
here, not wanting to give too much space to that part of the
book. Otherwise, it represents what I care to save of my
work as a poet.

On one occasion I was able to produce an impeccable
translation—in dealing with the "Night Song of the Fish"
by the German poet, Christian Morgenstern:

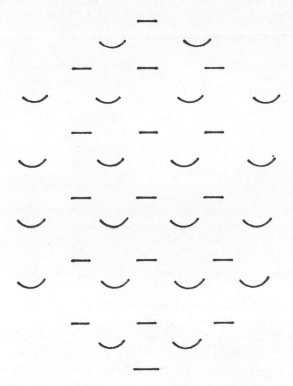

Here alone there was no question of balancing faithfulness to theme with faithfulness to form. In all other instances, where the differences between the two languages involved were such that the structure of the original could be presented together with its substance, I tried to do this. Thus, the rhymes in certain translations from Pasternak are the closest approximation that I could find to the apocopated off rhymes of the original. For the nuances, as well as for the prose sense, the metrics, and the rhyme schemes of the Russian poems, I am indebted to my husband, Avrahm Yarmolinsky. For help with the Japanese poems I am obliged to Kenneth Yasuda.

[xi]

For help with the Finnish lyrics I have to thank Sirpa Tuhkanen Yarmolinsky. These, like the poem by Walter Neumann, were among translations made with the aid of a Bollingen Foundation grant.

B.D.

ACKNOWLEDGMENTS

Most of the poems in this book were published in the following volumes, to which the author holds copyright: *Banners; Honey Out of the Rock; Fire for the Night; One Part Love; Take Them, Stranger; Animal, Vegetable, Mineral; Coming of Age; Collected Poems, 1919–1962.*

"Lament for the Makers : 1964" and "The Prepared Piano" originally appeared in *The Atlantic Monthly;* copyright has been assigned to the author. The following poems originally appeared in *The New Yorker:* "Late Reflections", "Passage", "Fireworks", "Another Autumn", "Earliness at the Cape", "Small Colored Boy in the Subway", "Disasters of War : Goya at the Museum", "Seascape", "On the Avenue", "A Carol Out of Season"; copyright has been assigned to the author. The following poems originally appeared in *Poetry:* "Suspension", "Barges on the Hudson", "July Day", "Unearthly Toy", "The Net", "The Lotus", "Admonition", "The Mother", "Lizard at Pompeii", "Homage to John Skelton"; copyright has been assigned to the author. The following poems originally appeared in *Harper's Bazaar:* "Urban Pastoral", "Berkshire Afternoon", "Summer Poem", "Homage to Braque", "Octaves", "Mermaid Remembered"; copyright has been assigned to the author. The following poems originally appeared in the *Columbia University Forum:* "Electronic Concert", "Stranger than the Worst", "On First Eating Dolphin", "Tivoli : Copenhagen"; copyright has been assigned to the author. The last-named poem also appeared in *Karen Blixen,* Gyldendal, Copenhagen. "N.Y. Tanka" originally appeared in *The Nation,* as did "e. e. cummingsesq", which was a review of Cummings' *50 Poems;* copyright has been assigned to the author. "A Day in Late August" appeared in *The Saturday Review;* copyright has been assigned to the author. "Space Man", "The Disenchanted", "A View of the Piazza di San Marco" appeared in the *transatlantic review* and are reprinted by permission of the publishers. "Coming of Age", read as the Phi Beta Kappa poem at Columbia University in 1957, is reprinted by permission of the *Prairie Schooner.* "Piano Recital" and "Reflections in a Little Park" first appeared in *New Poems by American Poets,* #1, edited by Rolfe Humphries, Ballantine Books, 1953, and are reprinted by their permission. "For Dylan Thomas on the Day of his Death", first published in the *Yale Literary Magazine,* appeared subsequently in *A Garland for Dylan Thomas* (Clarke & Way, 1963); copyright is held by the author. "Heard in Old Age" and "Voices on Riverside" are reprinted from *The Beloit Poetry Journal;* "Homage to Picasso, Sculptor", published in *The Literary Review;* "At the Green Grocer's, IV" is reprinted from *The Grécourt Review;* "At the Green Grocer's, V" and "Damnation" are reprinted from *The Compass Review.* "Cézanne" is reprinted from *Portfolio.* "Design", originally published in *Botteghe Oscure* under the title "A Villanelle", was subsequently reprinted in *Poetry Handbook,* by Babette Deutsch (Funk & Wagnalls, 1957).

"Tanka" and "Haiku" were originally published in *Poetry Handbook,* by Babette Deutsch (Funk & Wagnalls, 1957). "Quatrain" appeared in *Rogue's Legacy,* by Babette Deutsch (Coward, McCann, 1942) and is reprinted by their permission. "John the River" was first published in *The Kenyon Review* and also in *Jean Sans Terre,* by Yvan Goll (Thomas Yoseloff, 1958), as was "Landless John Salutes the Harlem River". "Come to the Park" (George), "Morgue" (Benn), "Spanish Dancer" (Rilke), and "Night Song of the Fish" (Morgenstern) are reprinted from *Contemporary German Poetry,* chosen and translated by Babette Deutsch and Avrahm Yarmolinsky (Harcourt, Brace, 1923), copyright in which is held by the author. "In All These Things", "Put Out My Eyes", "Although, as from a Prison", "You Are the Future" are from *Poems from The Book of Hours,* by Rainer Maria Rilke, translated by Babette Deutsch, copyright 1941 by New Directions, and are reprinted by permission of the publishers. The original of "Pause in the Firing" appeared in *Merkur,* Nr. 163; the translation is printed by permission of the author, Walter Neumann. The following translations appeared in *Two Centuries of Russian Verse,* edited, with an Introduction by Avrahm Yarmolinsky, translations from the Russian by Babette Deutsch, copyright 1949, © 62, 65, 66 by Avrahm Yarmolinsky (Random House, 1966): "My Country" (Lermontov); "Start of Long-Range Bombing", "Epilogue to *Requiem*", "From THE ORIENTAL NOTEBOOK" (all by Anna Akhmatova); "From *A Cloud in Pants*" originally published as "From *A Cloud in Trousers*", (Mayakovsky); "The Urals for the First Time", "Three Variations", "If Only, When I Made My Debut", "March" (all by Pasternak); "Hours of Sleeplessness" (Mandelshtamm); "The Foreigner" (Yevtushenko); "Ovidiopolis" (Martynov); and are reprinted by permission of the publishers. "For the Sake of the Thundrous Valor" is reprinted from the same volume; thanks are due to Mr. R. N. Grynberg for permission to reprint the translation of this poem by Mandelshtamm, the original of which appeared in *Aerial Ways,* edited and published by R. N. Grynberg. "Grapes" and "Here's Winter" appeared in *Two Centuries of Russian Verse;*

they were published earlier in *The Works of Alexander Pushkin*, edited by Avrahm Yarmolinsky (Random House, 1936) and are reprinted by permission of the publisher. The original of "Orpheus 7" (Eeva-Liisa Manner) appeared in her book: *Orfiset Laulut*, published by Kustannusoy Tammi. The original of "A Fragment of Sky" appeared in *Runoja*, 1961; the translation is printed by permission of the author, Tuomas Anhava. "Moses" was published in the *Columbia Forum*.

CONTENTS

[xviii]

V

VI

VII

LIGHT VERSE, OCCASIONAL POEMS, JUVENILIA

VIII

TRANSLATIONS

[xxi]

I

NEW POEMS

STRANGER THAN THE WORST

London Bridge was built
In a foggy century;
Men without anger or guilt
Shed blood to mortise the stones:
A child's. Year upon year,
Under a hotter sky,
Men brutish with fear
Wrenched a child's heart, throbbing,
Out of its cage of bones,
Screening with boisterous chants
The shrieks, the final moans.

To a woman in old age
Nothing of this is strange.
She knows the idolater's rage.
She thrills with the victim's pain.
In her own breast she keeps
A child, like the heart in its cage.
Sacrifice hardly sleeps,
Rousing again, as always,
To freshen a blackened stain.
The passionate innocent
Cries out, appalled. In vain.

Yet there is something comes
And goes, but comes again—
Emboldening, like drums,
But with the light grace of song,
And stranger than the worst.
Pure blitheness, out of the scums
Of evil and anguish will burst
Into a glory that
Dazzles beyond all wrong.
Love, as the old know love.
Fibred with grief, it is strong.

[3]

ELECTRONIC CONCERT

Music proposes. Sound disposes.
Under the thunders, under the bald swagging thunders, music
    has crumbled.
Before, behind, around, concussion stumbles on
Concussion, grumbling off
Into a boundless blindness.
Hurricane winds sweep through the skyscrapers,
Their shrieks of destruction cannot
Confound like the following silence.
Some demon's child is running, is banging on giant,
    invisible, impalpable iron railings.
Gurgles. Slurps. Far off, in angry trees
Rooks caw, hoarse as the unoiled casters of heavy furniture
    shoved across naked floors.
And then the sea. Sibilance greyly pushes
Against a shore that knows no night
But never saw a dawn.
Nearer, on the right, lunching termites are munching famous
    stone.
Beyond, above, as vastly empty as a Chirico landscape, hell's
    bowling-alleys
Resound: clock-voiced balls clattering
In discord with inhuman laughter.
When will the Machine create man in Its image?
Sound is many sands. The desert speaks.

LAMENT FOR THE MAKERS : 1964

Those black shoes broken in for the burial
At Drumcliff, MacNeice grew inured to: they were old
When he wore them to the burial in Laugharne.
Now he will not stoop again to pull on his shoes:
He, too, is buried. And if a bird of gold
Begins to sing? Snow falls where roses blow? Or a stale fern
Seeds? Then these deaths are mocked apocryphal news.

The deaths are mocked by the work. But the work is
    finished
With the lives and the minds that shaped it. Punctual as bills,
Though more like receipts, the books on Yeats arrive.
But not one poem by the poet arrives. The masks
His proud hands lifted gaily, the stubborn skills
Are lost. His folly, his rage, his esctasy survive
In lines the young man envies, in a question the scholar asks.

Too, that vain Bard, first famished and then battered
By tragic circumstance, who yet brimmed his verse
With a Virgilian calm—he does not twinkle now
At the Dog Star, twinkling. Frost's gone. And before him
    went
Four more; who, all but one, would laugh, all but one, curse:
Stevens. Fearing. Jeffers. e.e.c.—How
Believe that what each left was his last testament?

And what was Stevens'? Again from his ivory tower
He invites us to look down with him at the dump
And surveying, savor with his fruition the spread
Feast—of being, of poetry, sordor, radiance.
He offers hilarity, birdsong and rock, offers the glittering
    trump
Of summer's triumph, then the grave peace shed,
Saluting the quietus of the dance.

Next, his friend, Williams. Let him show you, my country-
    men,
How to perform a funeral, his own.
The hearse open, weathered, wheels fresh gilt, or none.
No flowers; behind the plain coffin all the mourners walk.
He was an American: his ancestors English, Dutch, French,
    even, as is known,
A Jew. Not strange that this poet should live on like one,
With sparrows keener than Yeats's eagle, tougher than Jeffers'
    hawk.

The animals haunting Roethke were minimal creatures:
Toad, newt, slug, elver; "the ugly of the universe"
Rejoiced that anxious heart, like every lovely thing:
The dazzling finch, roses, the dance of love. Though night
Shuddered with anguish that deepest horrors nurse,
From the abyss he cried, and crying, he would sing,
His gross body stretched toward—look!—a quenchless light.

Lament for the makers; it will never be over.
Dante could not believe death had undone
So many; since he said so, how many has death undone?
How many will death take tomorrow, or this year, certainly?
Dunbar made his lament over Chaucer and Henrysoun
And Walter Kennedy. Now we must make our own.
There is no end to grief. Nor no end to poetry.

HOMAGE TO BRAQUE

Your poésie: flowers on packing-cases;
birds, unidentifiable, in piercing flight;
mute eyes of fish flat on a plate; your studios
aggressively cluttered; your benches like guitars
in parks or urban gardens; your toreadors;
your stern Athena, mocked gently by the gentlest of grasses,
    make
—with their skew shapes, their nourishing colors:
the olive greys and greens, sunflower yellows,
the zenith azures, bloodred scarlets, hues
of stone, of sand, of sap, of various light—
make a world. Braque's. To give this, refreshes
the world, that poor poésie, where we too live.

OCTAVES

In the tiny island palace
The amber room of the Empress
Is elegant, harmonious.
The park in November, richer
By millions of leaves' late embers:
Maples' withering gold, oaks' bronze,
Burnt umber of elms—announces
A splendor no empress commands.
The splendor, recurrent, transient,
Of imperial autumn.

MERMAID REMEMBERED

Not on a rock, combing her sunbright hair (she's dark as
    Spain),
No seas foam round her tail,
This mermaid, small as a snail, perched
On a crystal shelf,
Is singular among her singular kind.
The guitar that her arms cradle is larger than herself.
She gazes, nor needs to sing,
But silently, tinily, mockingly
Enchants.
And after years, years,
Like music undersea, haunts fantasy.
Buried now in some museum cellar,
Distant as heart-parted lovers are,
This captive blackhaired fish-tailed inch of girl
With her unplucked guitar
Is yet the daughter of music, of the waters
(Whence Venus rose, they say, Venus
Who still returns, invisibly,
Imperishably).

THE PREPARED PIANO

(for John Cage)

It knocks. Does it knock? What knocks?
Neither grief nor joy.
                A whisper
plunders what never was heard
by a piano before.
Perhaps a mechanical bird,
                not Byzantine, not of gold,
yet a wonder, sings
              in a cold hall
of a thing
           never seen by the eyes
of a piano before.
Has the instrument gone daft?
               Can it know what is meant?
Or is it intent only
on what is learned by laughter?
              earned by
surprise? Surprise!
Surprise!

HOMAGE TO PICASSO, SCULPTOR

The cock, and bull, women, violins,
the goat. Every emblem of gism, of joy
moves, marches, cries, thrusting in bronze,
in copper overlaid
with colored paper, in wire, in straw, in
bronze, bronze, bronze, bronze.
Potency's resonance sculptured here
as form, as face, as animal or esprit.
The old man has a vigor beyond his youth, keener
because dying nears.
The final day, or night,
when the throat must gulp the last
parched instant.
Then he can make no more.
Then, moving, thrusting, crying, there will blaze
the cock, and bull, women, violins,
the goat.

MOSES

Old age is false as Egypt is,
And, like the wilderness, surprises
With inconceivable beauty that is like snow.
Now I am old, who was fed on promises,
Not always the same, not all nourishing,
But the great Promise was made to me, and
To my people, made by my God
And the God of my fathers, of Abraham,
Isaac, and Jacob.
                        He who is not seen,
But who beacons, as a pillar of cloud by day,
A pillar of fire by night.
Who is heard
                from a bush burning, or beside a rock,
A dry rock which, being struck, gushes water;
Who is heard on mount Zion, giving the law
Of life and knowledge.
But however heard or felt, is the unknown God.
As long as the heavens remain,
The unsearchable I AM.

Now an old man, I who fed on promises
Chew on memories as tough as thorn.
                                    I remember, though,
Boyhood was not all bad:
To be the plaything of the Pharaoh's daughter,
A Jewboy, but her darling: a soft life
Yet an uneasy one, that could not last.
It was a hard thing in those days to be a Jew.
Once when I was a young man, walking alone
Beyond the palace grounds, I saw
Slaves working, Jews, the overseer
Using his whip

On a Jew's back,
                    lashing him back and breast.
I was young then, my strength huge as my rage.
I killed the man.
                    I went into hiding,
Fled to Midian, found a wife
In one of Jethro's daughters,
Who bore me a son, me, a stranger
In a strange land.

Where I kept Jethro's flock.
Until on a day I led them beyond the desert
To the mountain of God, to Horeb.
                              There
I saw a bush on fire.
It was burning but it was not consumed.
I hid my face. I could not close my ears.
From the fiery bush God
Called, called me,
Moses, to deliver His people
Out of the hand of the Egyptians,
To bring forth the children of Israel out of Egypt.

Memories as tough as thorn.

I led His people
Through the wilderness forty years.
Famine, thirst, bone-weary travail,
War, sickness, murmuring, anger.
And Aaron died on mount Hor,
Nor saw Canaan. Forty years.
I, too, shall die soon. I shall not enter
The promised land.

It was given me to follow
The Lord, a pillar of cloud by day,
By night a pillar of fire.
Who shall never be known.

[13]

It was given me to hear
The law of life and knowledge.
To bring down the law to His people
From the One who shall not be named,
But shall be called only
I AM.

I shall not cross Jordan.
Not enter Canaan.
I shall see it, my old eyes are not dim,
Nor my force too much abated, from mount Nebo.
There it will be shown me—
The land of Gilead, as far as Dan,
All Naphtali, and the land of Ephraim,
Manasseh, and all the land of Judah

                      to the utmost sea.
The south, and the plain of the valley of Jericho,

                      the city of palm trees,
As far as Zoar.
But I shall not go over thither.
Shall be held in the land of Moab, where I shall be buried.

It is a hard thing to come so far,
After so long to be denied entrance.
This is a pang men after me will know.
Yet if I could enter, would I not
Be otherwise deprived?
I ask, what land—ah, Canaan!—can fulfill the promise
Of the Unsearchable?

TO PO CHÜ-I

In exile, alone,
Touching the strings of your instrument, soon falling silent;
Drinking alone;
Nibbling at the remembrance
Of distant festivals:
The flowery halls
Ringing with song, the feasts,
The dancing girls;
The prizes
From august imperial hands;
In exile, hungering after
Long gone hours with friends never again to be seen;
Thirsting after
Hours of talk that warms like wine, and for the wine cups
    with it
(Even Confucius, moderate in all things, was not so in
    drinking);
You knew again and again the grief of separation,
Knew the misery of old age, its thin consolations,
But chiefly the pangs of parting . . .

Now once more earth is shaken
With war and civil wars.
Men lie in exile
Gnawing the stones of privation
Till they die.
Yet in this wilderness of gaping graves
We open our hearts
To the knock
Of a thousand-year-old sorrow.

II

TO A DANCER

You are laughing as you run
To toss a ball in the sun;
And you'll pillow your head
Beside the incurious dead?

EPHEMERIS

Above the river, heavy with summer, air
Hangs sleepily,
Where in the embrace of afternoon
We lie, dumb as that air with our delight.
The grass is good to smell:
We suck the fresh
White ends of it, and this green place
Seems pleasanter for the taste.
Below, their shoutings half song, boys
Fling wild through the water; far away
A ripple gleams: laugh of a hidden
Child at play. And after,
Stillness is pointed by a stir in the leaves,
While through the leaves the sky
Blazes, intolerably blue.
Golden the haze is, from whose abundance we weave
A summer fugue:
Music that grieves for nothing.
Quietly
Day fails, the grass darkens.
A widening hush
Allows barely the shadow of an alas.
We stay only to watch the wimpling river flowing greyly on.

DEATH OF A CHILD

Are you at ease now,
Do you suck content
From death's dark nipple between your pale lips?
Now that the fever of the day is spent
And anguish slips
From the little limbs,
And they lie lapped in rest,
The young head pillowed soft upon that iron breast.
No, you are quiet,
And forever.
Though for us the silence is so loud with tears,
Through which we hear the dreadful-footed years
Echoing, but your quick laughter never,
Never your stumbling run, your sudden face
Thrust brightly scornful of our doubts and fears.
Now the dark mother holds you close.—Oh, you
We loved so,
How you lie,
How strangely still, unmoved how utterly,
Most dear, yet a little alien, too.

OMBRES CHINOISES

The city misted in rain, dim wet flashes of light
Strike through the dusk; vague thunderings—a train.
Over the street's glimmer the cabs rattle and slip;
Darkly the pavement's shine
Reaches into the night.
On blackness color flames: purple and blurs of red
Like fruits of faery bloom,
Yellow soft as honey and gold,
Green as though crushed emeralds bled,
Arctic blue in pale cold ribbons
Lost in fume.

Wind, and those shaken lanterns are swept off
By the shadows' broom.

"TO AN AMIABLE CHILD"

*On upper Riverside Drive, New York,
there is an enclosure containing a child's
grave. It is marked by a funerary urn,
the base of which bears this inscription:
"Erected to the Memory of an Amiable
Child, St. Claire Pollock. Died 15 July 1797,
in the Fifth Year of His Age."*

Was it because you'd wear
Your half-grown wisdom with a
Debonair gaiety, and laughed less than you smiled?
Or because you were tolerant
Of rainy days, of games and company you did not want?
I see you stilly radiant,
And—like delicious food, delicious play—
Loving music and motion and
Pleasure you did not understand
In voice or face or golden weather;
But sometimes for whole hours together
Hooding yourself in silence;
And when you tired of being good,
Driving them wild.
Could you go with death, making no outcry
If slow-footed, as though with nurse at bedtime?
You lie alone here.
Turfs and a quaint urn
Cover the dust of your small body.
The show
Of your inimitable ways is over.
Child, amiable centuries ago,
At your city-huddled little grave
You are remembered so:
Haunting too merrily for a ghost, you are loved
Now.

DISTANCE

Two pale old men
Sit by a squalid window playing chess.
They are ignorant
Of the street's clamorousness as children
Bent absorbed over their toys.
The old heads nod.
A parchment-colored hand
Hovers above the board.
Shrewd schemes are woven, where they sit
So still;
Ravelled, reknit once more with laboring skill.
When "check" is said, huskily, a point is scored
For one whose eyes flicker as if a jest
Lit them, his beard lifts a moment
And then sinks on his thin chest.
Within the dark, warped window-frame
Heavily they rehearse
The old designs:
Two rusty skull-caps bowed
Above the game that now lets them forget
Their pains,
Their deaths,
Shut safe and proud within
The grandeur of its abstract universe.

BALLET SCHOOL

Fawns in the winter wood
Who feel their horns, and leap,
Swans whom the bleakening mood
Of evening stirs from sleep,
Tall flowers that unfurl
As a moth, driven, flies,
Flowers with the breasts of a girl
And sea-cold eyes.
The bare bright mirrors glow
For their enchanted shapes.
Each is a flame, and so,
Like flame, escapes.

SEPTEMBER

This is the month when sun and wind contend
For the possession of that lapis, thinned
To milkiest opal, that is pure bare sky.
A cloud-puff is a milkweed soberly
Shredded by breezes with the fists of boys.
Only to breathe the air is to grow wise
On a transparent liquor, to grow still
As the unherded ruminants who kneel
On the horizon as against a wall—
The hornless hills that want nor barn nor bell.
A butterfly drifts down without a sound,
Proving it is no leaf of sudden brown
To whisk along the floor. The boughs, the turf,
Hug their thick green as though it were a scarf
Against adventuring chill. Few and small,
The russet tongues of the barberry thrill
The hairy verdure with a tinge of fire.
Now apple-seeds grow black, now seeds of pear;
Now the grapes tighten; meadows shake like seas,
And rivers are more level than the fields.
Shadows lie late, their long, drowsy limbs
Spread on the grass; before dusk falls, the winds
Cease, with all noises but the crickets' din;
Poor death's asleep, and we'll not waken him.

SUN BATH

Clothed in languor and nothingness
Lie, and feel the summer press
Her molten seal of hot bright gold
On cheek, on flank; lie still and hold
Hills at arm's length, and watch the sky
Like an ethereal sea reel by;
Watch the boughs' rich plumage turn
To solitary greens that burn;
Shrink human nerves to comprehend
How tentative antennae bend;
Stretch human powers to converse
With ghosts of giants, who rehearse
An unearthly drama there
On the blue platform of the air.
So dissolve into the mood
Of slow, sun-fired, sun-soothed blood
That the huge earth and the heart
Move without stop as without start
In one firm rhythm—being, be
Apprenticed to felicity.

MOVING

After the fretful hours were done—
Morning, noon, and afternoon,
After dusk had come, too soon,
And the sun,
A flushed, speechless creditor,
Upon our lack
Had turned a hasty back,
I turned my own
Upon small swarming trifles and edged fears,
To face their residue from other years.

Going from an old house to a new
Gives one curious things to do—
Closets to empty,
Heartaches to throw away,
Threadbare joy
To divest of mothballs,
Papers to destroy:
Letters from golden lads and girls who say
They have come home from the university
With nothing learned but what they were not taught,
Or, they are in love again,
Or, they are sad
Because of too little love and too much thought,
Or, asking what was meant on such a day
When a certain person said
The sort of thing people will say . . .
It doesn't matter.
Some of them are dead,
And some are married, and a few
Are famous.
Going from an old house to a new
Gives one tiring things to do.

And when we leave that new house, as we must,
Maybe, after some yet unlived years,
Shall I look back
To this night, and call myself a fool
For having cried in my heart for the old school
And the university
And the lovers and friends
Lost in the dark forest of the world?
Ambitions shrink;
Time pulls the best awry;
And ends
Come harder as we grow older.
The nights grow colder—
Or do I?

"WHAT'S PAST IS PROLOGUE"

An April Paris brought again
The sweet selfish stingless pain
Of younger springtimes, ignorant of
The poverty of proven love.
Evening, moving through the heat
And dust of the bright noisy street,
As one half goddess and half whore
Waited at the open door.
Laying quiet on the air
Like a fresco's floating hair,
She squeezed the heart as milkmaids squeeze
The udder caught against their knees.
Evening passed, and night came on,
Lighting softly, one by one,
Stars like arc-lamps in a town
Viewed from an airship upside down.
Night came on, who had no share
In pain that is unmixed with care,
The pain of springtimes ignorant of
The poverty of love.

"THE LAURELS ALL ARE CUT"

We'll to the woods no more, for now
The winter of delight is here:
Earth stony as the fabled moon,
The sky lean-faced, as withering soon,
Rains cannot warm the damnèd bough
Where sits the gutter chanticleer.

There was a season when we walked
In meadows that were dim with blue
And violet life our sharp heels bruised.
The ground kept what the heavens refused
Of color, and a tall wind stalked
Beside us, gathering handfuls, too.

And when the blue was lost there came
A scattered scarlet in its stead.
The grass grew staunchly round each nest
Where sun-fed berries, breast to breast,
Nestled as bright as tropic flame,
And we drank honey where they bled.

These gone, there was a month as bright
As dreams of India to the West
Before the land of gold was snared.
The field lay still, its russet-haired
Warm pelt stroked smooth by drowsy light,
Till the sun slept, and dark was best.

We'll to the woods no more, for now
The winter of delight is here.
But in our blood the summer cries
Compassion on the bird that dies
And leaves no ghost upon the bough
To chill with song the sluggish year.

[31]

QUANDARY

There is no shelter anywhere
For her whose wonder, like a hare,
Bursts through the briars of despair,
And bleeds and leaps away.
There is no cave where she may keep.
The stream she drinks of is too deep
For her to ford. Her little sleep
The dreadful stars betray.

The panther heart within her breast
Will never drum her pain to rest,
Who so much fears to be possessed
By tyrannous circumstance.
Though she but stands, she seems to flee,
She trembles so to be as free
As if she'd shed mortality,
And smiled at her own trance.

How to sustain the miracle
Of being, that like a muted bell,
Or like some ocean-breathing shell,
Quivers, intense and still?
How close to her the golden room
That the world builds of its own gloom?
Her patient, furtive, fertile doom
Is there no way to kill?

FOR THE INFANT MICHAEL

Sweet, where music softly goes
Toward silence, and upon that bed
Sleeping, is rememberèd:
Where the breathing of the rose
Defines a fragrance halfway fled:
Or from wintry wings unshed
Hover rumours of the snows:
In such hushed, such honey-holding,
Subtle ways your being runs,—
O virgin bud be slow, unfolding
A radiance like the sun's.

THE PARTY

In the blonde room the lustrous-limbed piano,
Like an incarnate shadow with heart and nerves,
Seems to wait for those fleshly apparitions
Whose passing humors it so darkly serves.

They come: the room contracts with talk and gesture;
Its pictures pale as they nod with curving cheeks;
They flutter the music score with debating fingers.
The keyboard smiles like a wise old slave—and speaks.

Their voices rise and float, wreathing, dissolving
Over the resolute, quivering instrument.
Touch and kiss, grave-flower, wine-drenched laughter
Bloom in a fountain of sound, fade like a scent.

The music gutters at last, is snuffed like a candle.
Gay gossip follows, feasting . . . The farewells start.
Alone in the ash-blonde room the dark piano
Stands like a shining shadow with nerves and heart.

III

LINES WRITTEN IN TIME OF PEACE

What shall we do with country quiet now?
A motor drones insanely in the blue
Like a bad bird in a dream.

Hush.
The giant plane roars
Gently as a carrier pigeon, soon
Drowned in the distance.

Before the shadows have engrossed the grass
There is a patch of sun to lie upon—
The pale warm thing that summer sheds
When she's ready to be gone.
The peaceful fragrance has not passed
From the fleece that she has worn.
The full bough, the bush, the dreaming vine
Vie with lush greens. To what should grief
Open its eyes again?

One leaf, blood-bright, stains quiet
Like a cry.

The child's cough scratches at my heart—my head
Buzzes with rumors of war, bad news
From China, stories of men bred
In ant-hills that will overthrow the world.
Hens can turn into cocks now, if we choose.
Machines can split the atom, it is said.
Thoughts are hurled
East, west, up and down the universe.
But few so dizzying as the sitting still,
In lamplight, among friends
(The cough's no worse?),
And watching eyes beam, lips part: warmth, wit, skill,
Feasting each other . . .
Oh, keen, oh, kind!
Here time undoes itself while we review
Those rare beginnings that have fortunate ends,
Rehearse a drama equal to the mind.
Say children cry, with reason,
And men die
Unreasonably, say our hearts are torn
And our brains puzzled—we face
Miracles. Not the halved atom, not the changeling bird,
But this, this short moment of human grace
That for long pain can strangely make amends.

SCARECROW

A queer dark shape to scare
Nothing on that bright street,
In the sharp glittering air,
He kept his broken feet
Still, so to save them, while
His coat flapped in the wind.
And, as girls will beguile
Vexed heart or perplexed mind,
The rusty figure wound
And unwound rapidly
A bit of thread he'd found
And clutched at thriftily—
A trick cold fingers caught
Quickly, a thing to do.
His eyes were bare of thought.
His foot stared through his shoe.
A flapping shape to scare
None but himself, where grain
Was none to guard, his care
Was but to wind again
And then again unwind
His bit of thread, not more
Than any scarecrow blind
To what he did it for.

THE SONG

Oh, bitter-hearted me, thrice-parted me,
What Pythagorean discipline will wring
From discord, harmony?
And where, out of this quarreling breast,
Shall peace be found?
Neither the earth, the bloody-syllabled,
Nor the distracted air
Affords a ground
For music to build house.
Selves, you are blackguards who inhabit me
As vagabonds do ditches, prisoners—jails:
Bound, being at rest,
And muddied, being free.
Yet now, even with harsh cracked voices, sing,
Together sing,
And briefly, though joy fails,
Despair rejoices.

RECORD BY YVETTE GUILBERT

On the wall
Jan Avril
Flaunts violent stripes,
Bends her head
Too boldly for a dancer dead.
C'EST le mai!
Below, the slow revolving disc
Quickening gives out
A shout
That recalls
The bones, the jowls, the black gloves, the yellow gown
Set down with Toulouse-Lautrec's
Savage stroke.
C'est le MAI!
Who was it sang?
Who was it spoke?
Dancer, painter, old diseuse,
Anarchists and Fascists must
Come to dust,
But the rich
Malice, the gay lust refute
The tomb, the war, and the listeners, smiling silently
In the polite room.
C'EST LE JOLI MOIS DE MAI!

THE DISPASSIONATE SHEPHERDESS

Do not live with me, do not be my love.
And yet I think we may some pleasures prove
That who enjoy each other, in the haste
Of their most inward kissing, seldom taste.

Being absent from me, you shall still delay
To come to me, and if another day,
No matter, so your greeting burn as though
The words had all the while been packed in snow.

No other gift you'll offer me but such
As I can neither wear, nor smell, nor touch—
No flowers breathing of evening, and no stones
Whose chilly fire outlasts our skeletons.

You'll give me once a thought that stings, and once
A look to make my blood doubt that it runs.
You'll give me rough and sharp perplexities,
And never, never will you give me ease.

For one another's blessing not designed,
Marked for possession only of the mind,
And soon, because such cherishing is brief,
To ask whereon was founded the belief

That there was anything at all uncommon
In what each felt for each as man and woman—
If this then be our case, if this our story,
Shall we rail at heaven? Shall we, at worst, be sorry?

Heaven's too deaf, we should grow hoarse with railing,
And sorrow never quickened what was failing.
But if you think we thus may pleasures prove,
Do not live with me, do not be my love.

WINE PARTY

As coins because they shine
Remain unspent,
The golden-bodied wine
Will first content
The pure lust of the eye.
Enough, if such rich lustre pay the sight
With interest upon long vanished light.

This pleasure as it pales
Seems not so fine
As what the glass exhales:
Breath of the vine.
Rare gust, be slow to die!
We'll take it on the tongue: mixed with our breath
The ghostly grape laughs jollily at death.

The wine, though cool as snow,
Being drunk, is fire.
The taste transmutes the glow,
Until desire
Puts its long grieving by,
Or finds some savor of sweetness in what's tart.
Though wrung, the heart exults, the shuddering heart.

The failure of delight
That makes us rage,
The treachery, the spite
Of this fouled age,
Wine's power can defy.
The blood bounds in the vein, flesh unsubdued
Forgets its pain, the soul forgets its solitude.

CREATURES IN THE ZOO

APE

His eyes are mournful, but the long lined palm
He thrusts between the bars expects the best.
His old man's face as innocent as calm,
The beggar puts compassion to the test
And fails. He grips the bars; his pained stare grows
To a brown study framed in dusty fur.
He has a cold. He sneezes, cleans his nose,
Then gravely licks a flexile forefinger.

A pause; the bald mauve hand from which men shrink,
The fingers, strong to clutch, quick to explore,
Again extended, are again refused.
The eyes, poor sorrow's jewels, seldom wink,
But to his grinning public, as before,
Show endless patience, endlessly abused.

YOUNG GAZELLE

Stiff as her Egyptian counterpart
Standing on legs of matchstick ivory,
She hides the racing of her heart,
While the black boss of her enormous eye
Flames inconsolable. Less like a deer
Than like a freckled girl, her skin's blanched gold
Drawn over little bones, her head held clear,
She listens, as if breathing were too bold.

A tremor, and she is still. Now sunny peace,
Light as the straw beneath her feet, persuades
Her pulses briefly. The terror goes—
Whipped by a childish whimsy of release,
She caracoles: a quick bound that evades
The bars. Then drops into a thrilled repose.

[44]

LIONESS ASLEEP

Content that now the bleeding bone be swept
Out of her reach, she lay upon her side.
In a blonde void sunk deep, she slept, she slept
Bland as a child, slept, breathing like a bride.
Color of noons that shimmer as they sing
Above the dunes, her sandy flanks heaved slow.
Between her paws curled inward, billowing
Waves of desert silence seemed to flow.

The crowd was gone, the bars were gone, the cage
Thinned into air, the sawdust and the fleas
Winnowed by sleep to nothing. After food,
Absence possessed her: bliss keener than rage,
If slumber's prisoner at a bound could seize
This ghostly freedom, lapping it like blood.

BLACK PANTHER

This little panther wears a coat of soot,
Well-suited so. Stretched out along his shelf,
Still as one brooding storm, the sultry brute
Looks soft as darkness folded on itself.
His limbs, his tarry torso, are as mat
As night wanting the stars; his resting grace
Lies leashed. Alone his head's erect: pure cat
Stares, alive with danger, in that face.

From the sharp ears down to the finest hair
At his tail's tip, he might be carved of coal.
Child of the shadows, he appears as tame,
Till, from behind the grate, the gold eyes glare
With such a light as could consume the whole
To ashes and a memory of flame.

[45]

TWO PEOPLE EAT HONEY

Beyond the window the moon may be in riot
With the winter night. But your voice having ceased
In the room here, silence comes, barefooted,
To cover the leavings of our frugal feast.
Your hands rest on the table, clasped, quiet.
Kind as a country servant, silence moves
About us, with a tender dignity smoothing
The unseemly creases in our loves.
Your eyes upon me change no more than the rooted
Shadow beside your chair. Your eyes know
Upon what song this night has locked her throat.
The melody trembles toward us, still too low
To name, though the music mounts above our breathing,
Mounts, and mingles with, far off, a train
That pants harshly of journeys. Your eyes upon me.
We are alone again.

AT THE BATTERY

Over the water, polished
Pitch bright in the darkness,
The funnel dipping, the lantern
Swinging: yellow, a stripe
Falling across the cabin's
Cosy shabbiness, cutting
Out of the shadows a worn
Face, and a blackened pipe.

Soft incessant insistent
Puffs of steam in the offing.
Close, on the quay, a sailor
Turns an indifferent stare
From his business of pumping;
Water flushes the planks, and
Ceasing, quiet swallows
The simple scene like air.

No more. This was sufficient
To give fabulous midnight
Earnest intimate glory.
River and lantern webbed
The men, the tug, the moorage
In a steady fluxion,
As the heart swelled, throbbing,
The short hour ebbed.

NEED

What do we need for love—a midnight fire
Flinging itself by fistfuls up the chimney
In soft bright snatches? Do we need the snow,
Gentle as silence, covering the scars
Of weeks of hunger, years of shabby having?
Summer or winter? A heaven of stars? A room?
The smiling mouth, the sadness of desire
Are everywhere the same. If lovers go
Along an unknown road, they find no less
What is familiar. Let them stay at home,
And all will still be strange. This they know
Who with each heartbeat fight the fear of change.

DOGMA

Love is not true: mathematicians know
Truth, that's alive in heaven, and in the mind—
Out of our bodies; you will never find
Love strict as number, and enduring so.
It is not free: alone the grave's narrower
Than the little space in which this passion moves,
With a door that opens inward: he who loves
Measures his paces like a prisoner.

They who give it large names are liars, or
They are fools. More softly, you and I,
Slow to assert what we can never prove,
Wonder what algebraist, what dictator
Can teach us much of truth or tyranny.
Look at me. Do not speak. But this is love.

TRURO HOUR

Carved by the stillness, clean as rock
The moors lie open to the sky.
Each bearded dune stands like a stock
In early nudity.
No shadow stirs, to crack the spell
Cast by the heat upon this waste
That shows the candor of a shell
To heavens as bare, as chaste.
Alone coarse beach grass, shaggy pine
Find sea-grudged root beneath the sand,
And stubborn as the wind, define
The salt lagoon from the salt land.
White as the surf, white as the sun,
The cottages cling sleepily
Each to its hillock, one and one,
Like sea-fed gulls beside the sea.
Between its knees this naked place
Holds the strange peace that is assured
To those who smile in their embrace
At violence dreaded or endured.

MEMORY POISED

As on the throat of some museum piece,
On this chaste air is inlay of gold leaf,
Quieter there
Than sun on cheek, abstract as emperor's jewel
Cased in glass, truer than enamel.
Tumult of swollen waters on the rocks
Below, remote as rare,
Exalts a sovereign stillness.
Balancing
Stiff leaf and stubborn wave,
The tug chugging, the enormous
Strain of the delicate piers, the cloud, the light,
And cinders on the track behind,
The hour
Is silverly suspended.

Insecure, lay this upon some high shelf of the mind,
Not for the eyes
But for the heart to come
Back to, reclaim, and, more than art, admire:
Memory poised
In vulnerable, proud equilibrium.

SUB SPECIE AETERNITATIS

Look up to the clear arc: bodilessly
Climb
The ridge-pole of heaven,
Swing through the blue tent
Burning with tall cold.
No wind
Breathes
On the brimming peace.
But to perfect
Time's truce—
Single, gold, one leaf
Swerves to the ground.
One crane
Like a slow arrow through the hollow air
Moves truly,
Never to be seen again.

INSUFFICIENCY

What though the moon pours restlessness?
The stars in unison are uttering peace.
The trees are shapes of stillness that no wind,
No birdy shift, rouses from their dark trance.
If there's a soul of stature to address
The night's hugeness, it asks no release.
But one that is ragged, one that is lame and blind
Shudders to hear the silent heavens dance.

Dispersed and spent,
As in legend the limbs of Osiris
Crying one to another, the unknowing undying
Scattered limbs of the god:
On the winter waters
Lie
The hand without fingers,
The feet without speed,
The head without thought, the torse hacked and adrift
And its heart in a house without windows
Beaten upon by the sea,
Unknowing, undying.

Where were you then, my sister, my soul?
Seeking
Through the two kingdoms, imploring
The Upper Region, the Lower, getting no answer?
Asking the birds of the sky
Who deceived you and vanished?
We called you,
We the sad limbs in dispersion.

In vain.

But flying you sought us.
The dead could not stop you.
No, nor the horns of Evil
Those that undid us.
And we cried, scattered.
Cried, and were mute.
And you came, O soul, my sister,
Flying, quick with compassion, the sleepless mother,
Unwearied bride.

Restored
To the hand its fingers, and speed to the feet,
And the heart
Beating again in the body, healed and made whole,
And the brow
Crowned with thought, lord of the nether kingdom.

Now, united,
Shall we not rule?
Can we forgive and govern?
You beside me, and I
That lately was many, scattered and tossing
On the horns of the
Savage dividing waters,
Can we endure?
Death under our sceptre. O
Sharper than death, unpersuadable Evil
Behind and before us?

Do not
Speak, mother and bride, my sister:
We that were
Scattered, now are made one,
We that were
Parted, now are at peace.
O do not
Lay a lightest feather upon the scales
Held in equipoise of triumphant stillness.
Now, my sister, my soul, requited, remember
As I, requited, foresee
The workings of Evil, past and to come.
Nor deny—
Denial only is dying—
This moment of union.

SUMMER SOLSTICE

Here in the lap of summer, in the silence
Sharpening every voice:
The bird's,
The boy's spiralling laughter,
Quiescence folds
Itself upon itself, like the blunt hills.
And grows,
No more mysterious than a flower states
Its color to the sun.
Here's a boy's joy
In the arrow that finds its mark.
But the man learns
Houndlike devotion to a universe
Whose evil is not measured, and whose careless
Unhoped-for love
Only dark patience earns.

IV

WINTER SOLSTICE

This is the winter wonder:
Leafless morning
Reigns in the cold street like a sycamore
Clothed in its leopard skin, the golden pallor
Blotting out shadow.
Yet the sore mind
Fumbles, biting on its memories
Like a trapped animal gnawing his caught
Limb;
Freed, must limp
Through war's enormous jungle, bleeding still.
Chill poultice of these wounds, too distant
Lies the bright silence of a polar day.
Only the eyes,
Enchanted by a wintry innocence,
Stay with the tree of light that shows no bud,
Pillar whose glory knows no compromise
With ripening or decay.

HISTORY

Once it was packed like a box with the toys of childhood,
Even the largest dolls grown small and familiar,
And the cuckoo clock saying,
"Tomorrow, tomorrow."
Once it was sad and comic like Mr. Punch,
And events jumped up, like Judy, to be whacked
Over the head, and the greatest kings, like actors,
Were happily at once dead and alive.
Once it was apart
As a crumbled castle on a darkening slope
Half seen from the express.
But whether it was tall as towers or
Tumbled with playthings on the nursery floor,
It was remote and faithful.

History
Coming too close
Is monstrous, like a doll
That is alive and bigger than the child
Who tries to hold it.
It is a clock that tolls the thirteenth hour.
It is a theatre
On fire.
Our history
Images not the castle but the train
Emerging from the tunnel, ruining
Down the embankment toward the modest station,
Where it will lie like a box of toys, broken,
Unpacked in vain.

TO MY SON

Now the blackout of frontiers
Between home and Gehenna
Kills the light in the eyes
That would speak to you, throttles
The word in the throat, estranges
Us from ourselves. Our soiled pledges
Lie among broken bottles for the ragpicker's sorting
When the bombers are still.

How shall we talk
To you who must learn the language
Spelled on the fields in famine, in blood on the sidewalk?
Child (shall I say?),
When the night roars, remember
The songs we sang, lapped in the warmth and bright
Of the nursery:
Malbrough s'en va t'en guerre
Ne sait quand reviendra.
Farewell and goodbye to you, Spanish ladies,
Farewell and goodbye to you, ladies of Spain.
Memory stifles thought
Where the lamp throws a stain on the floor.
Youth is the time to dance.
No more: we have lost your music.
The iron that rings the brain,
The weight in the hollow
Breast where the heart should beat,
Remain.

I cannot hide you now,
Or shelter you ever,
Or give you a guide through hell.
You are ignorant, you are unarmed, and behind your
Scornful smile you, too, are afraid.
History threatens you at each street corner,
The seas are sewed up, and the colors fade
On every map you studied early and well.

The driven exile discovers
Midway in an obscure wood
What does not bloom for the fool:
The flower whose root is despair.
You, in an obscure room in a masterless school,
Must find the faith that cements
The promises public events and private blunders have broken.

Are you alone?
This I would have you remember
(Who felt your heartbeat before you had breath to cry with):
You must wrestle alone
In the stony night like the Jew
Compelling the awful angel.
If you fight in the dark
With your self till you force a confronting,
You will be blessed in the morning.

You will be blessed recalling
The question you asked as a child:
How can I change myself
When I have nothing to change
My self with? Then I smiled,
Finding an answer: your will.
Now I know it is love of the impossible

That forms the dove and the lion.
It is love
Of the impossible
That brings the soul to its own.

Though I can hardly reach you and never prove
What the event will teach you,
I who am helpless to move
You from the road you choose,
Or alter the face you will meet there,
Leave you these words with my love.

1943

REFLECTION

Looking in time's long mirror
What image do you see?
One holding a golden basin
For the hands of authority.
We are haunted by the Roman
Face, ominous and tired,
As by the womanish gesture
Of one who has desired
To be free of choice: a burden
Too heavy for old men.
The image in the mirror
Reveals itself again.
The governor slowly washes
One hand with the other hand.
The soldiers wait, impassive,
Obedient as the sand.
We stare on that repeated
Scene till our eyeballs ache.
Will a sandstorm rise? Will the mirror
Crack? Will the image break?

DAWN IN WARTIME

Sunrise tumbling in like a surf,
A foam of petals, curling thousands, lightly crumbling
Away into light.
Waking to this, how could the eyes hold
The shape of night's barren island, the cold cliffs
Climbed in sleep, how
Recall the burned sore scabby
Face of the world?
Into that sea of light the spirit waded
Like a young child at morning on the beach,
Saw only those giant combers, soft as roses,
That mothy spume unfeathering into air.
Lingered there, as a child lingers
To smooth bastions of whitest sand,
To finger shells brighter than dogwood flowers,
To stand, quietly,
Watching the immense marvel of morning
Rolling toward him all its uncreated hours.

SOLITUDE

What is it comes at evening into the room?
When you are alone, when muted lamplight glosses
The wood, yellowing the page whose notes
Blackly assert a deaf man's agony:
The music that his ears cannot receive
Ever. Ever. What is here now?
What does the silence say?
And the books gravely coloring the walls,
Their wisdom shut between boards, behind glass,
Like an anonymous exile without passport.
What is it breathes
So the lamp flickers like a candle flame?
The music beats, as soundless as a heart,
Touching your heartlessness.
And the room widens to receive the night,
The shut page sparkles like a tear,
The deaf man's agony becomes your joy,
Death littles. O what clear
Crystal
Forms at evening in the lonely room,
The lover, like an enemy, can break!

THE PHOENIX

Staring in zoos at the dull-eyed and wild
Who never meet their gaze,
The child, the refugee, the idle sailor
Halt their wanderings to praise the plumage
Of every bird but this.
The friendless seaman and the exile trade
Feathered marvels for their memories.
The child escapes
To a safe jungle rich with cries and colors.
Comforted, they turn back
To the barred nursery, the bareness of
Shipboard or rented room.

Will you come, phoenix joy?

On the stained path two lovers pause.
The air
Throbs
Where upon no visible branch
His wings of light, his breast,
Softer than any kiss, an instant rest.
The world's worst shabbiness
Crumbles. Their eyes meet.

Would you fly, phoenix joy?

But these, returning
Late and alone, will hear the song he sings
Among the ashes as
His self-begotten beauty dying burns.

CITY PARK

The sun they seek unmasks their leisure, bares
Poverty in their clothing, in their hearts.
The loveless cripple, the warped ancient wears
Need like a badge. The glance each darts
At passers-by, like a child's arrow, blunt
And wanton, is retrieved again to fail.
Their patience does not find what it should hunt,
Where pigeons peck and a sparrow flits its tail.
They scarcely stir, sometimes their fingers fret
Their sleeves. The words they drop are buttons loosed
From a worn thread. Here, birdlike, they forget
The world of green beyond their urban roost.
Faithful as disappointment, they come back
With the bland light that placates as it numbs,
Sharpening their shadows to a narrower black
Among the drifted leaves and few stale crumbs.
And then a cold wind rises and the sun
Falters; they must move. Slowly, they go
Along the dusty path, becoming one
With dusk, that tells them only what they know.

THE BELVEDERE : MOZART'S MUSIC

Here on this hill, beyond the sick world's pain,
Landscape is legend, from the shadowy plain
To topknots blonde with sun and lakes that shine
Softly as bloom of porcelain or of wine.
The contours of this classic structure keep
The distance of a dream, where, mocking sleep,
They seem to dance, to vanish, to revive,
Strict as an archaic smile, and yet alive.
No architect on earth was ever skilled
As one musician so to plan and build
A tower true as only number is,
So firm in air, so blithe for view as this.
Most heavy heart, be lifted up, and come
To find yourself in heaven and at home.

THEN AND NOW

Then was the grown-up world of tall decision,
Its beauty of late nights denied a child;
World of bewildering gifts, and strange derision,
Alien alike whether it frowned or smiled,
Yet your least wish was governed by its laws.
The landscape and the weather both were odd,
Exploding with effects that hid a cause
Serene and lonely as the Will of God.
Recall it: peopled by an august race,
Immune to the passions that attack the young,
And knowing all. There every commonplace
Must be translated from a marvellous tongue.

Now is the world of grandeur dwindled, shrunk
To what the stupidest can understand.
The shabby treasures of an exile's trunk
Include no passport to that wonderland,
Though you are told you are a citizen.
The scenery is changed, the climate dull;
The fateful masks are faces, gods are men;
Most nights are long and few are magical.
But there are strangers even here: their speech
Is rich in barbarous mystery, their ways
Are private, who live wholly beyond reach,
Admired and feared, though none of us obeys
Their foreign rule. No dictators, and yet
Strong utterly. While we, with pity wrung
For what they must do, suffer, learn, forget,
Feel shy when we approach them. They are young.

THE NET

Into this net of leaves, green as old glass
That the sun fondles, trembling like images

In water, this live net, swung overhead
From branch to branch, what swam? The spider's thread

Is less passive, where it appears to float
Like a bright hair clinging to the wind's coat.

Hot at work, history neither schemes nor grieves
Here where the soaking dead are last year's leaves,

And over them slung, meshed with sun, a net
No creature wove, none frantically tried to fret.

The huge weight of time without its sting
Hangs in that greenly cradling woof. A wing

Has caught there, held. Held. But not to stay,
We know, who, how slowly, walk away.

A BULL

His sad brown bulk rears patient as the hills
Hunched like dark herders at the pasture's back.
Swaying, he will not topple like those clouds
Heavy with throttled thunders. Lust that thrills
The crowd, to see such power pricked and teased
Through hot blind plunges to a sandy death
While they breathe blood, rage flowering in their veins,
His poor tame suffering will not have appeased,
Who takes the sun's barbs in a sullen drowse.
The ritual of his fertility
Is simple; he was bred only to breed,
The homely husband to a score of cows.
Yet monstrous as a myth, his front denies
His humbled horns, as, hugely male, he stands
Hung with endurance as with iron weights.
Clustering flies mate round his red-rimmed eyes.

THE GULLS

On the steep cliff
That hung over the sand,
Where nothing moved for the eye's farthest reach
But ocean's royal colors twitched with white,
And, on the sky-wide beach, a flock of gulls,
I gave my joy into the birds' wild keeping.
On the shore
Only the gulls were living, and
Beyond, those lucid greens,
Those traveling purples, dark as fate.
I could believe the gulls more beautiful
Than Yeats's swans above the lake at Coole.
Fifty and more, by my uncertain count,
They rested there,
Till suddenly, upon what wind of impulse who could say,
They rose, as if the shore were answering
Ocean's harsh whisper with a grey salutation,
To settle on the sea.
They were at home, being wave-bred, on their wide
    watery nest,
And, floating quietly as clots of foam,
They rocked my joy with them upon that boundless breast.
But not for long.
Once more they rose, over fifty of them, away
In winged ellipse.
And as they flew,
Leaving the vast shore still, the vast sea bare,
I marveled that, though the gulls carried it
Viewless into the sky, poor human joy
Could rise so high, could, vanishing, stay.

NATURAL LAW

If you press a stone with your finger,
Sir Isaac Newton observed,
The finger is also
Pressed by the stone.
But can a woman, pressed by memory's finger,
In the deep night, alone,
Of her softness move
The airy thing
That presses upon her
With the whole weight of love? This
Sir Isaac said nothing of.

INTERLUDE

Accordion music meanders the pathless woods
From the hidden cabin like one lost, half sorry
To find his way home at last. Coolly, the sun,
With wind for helper, teaches the young forest
Basketry of shadow.
The accordion pauses, rests; the single noise
Is a grasshopper scraping his wing with his leg
On a bleached log.
Wasps weave through the silence
Now veined by the voice of a bird.
Sky holds fiery blue
In a green mosque of leaves. Here how all praises
The passing summer, and the sound almost fails
Of the seep of sunny moments.
As for defense, eyes look toward the tower
Of one formidable cedar,
While the hour bleeds twinkling away.

STRING QUARTET

Who have no heaven come
Into the hall that passively receives
Their fluttering chattering quotidian selves,
The grieving mind and the deceiving heart.
Then they recede, as who should bow before
The entering instruments.
These find their places,
And all is garden and is grace, is
Eden, animal and innocent.
The violins and the viola cradle restless chins,
The serious cello's blonde body glows.
How faithful are the dog-eared scores, and how
The bows lift, scenting music!
Now, coolly as a flower
Unfolds, paradise
Begins.
      Fingers prance on the strings,
      Bows dance in air,
      Time is undone even where time grows,
      Blossoming like a tapestry's blue and rose,
      Vanishing like its colors at day's close:
      Blossoming, fading, vanishing, only to spring
      Up as a fountain tossing a crystal ball
      On the tips of the water's fingers.
Will it roll away out of the hall:
The impalpable sphere striped with day and night,
Or tossed once more
Leap into the sky
And be lost?
Some cough, some sigh, or stir in their chairs,
Some stare
At the floor or the ceiling, a few close their eyes.

Time is the hairs of a horse stroking the gut of a sheep,
Time is a hole in the carpet, is dust on the lamp,
    is a cramp in the knee.
Time is nothing to see.
What is it summons
The son of the morning from this hollow wood
In his first radiance, summons
The daughters of music too in theirs?
What temporal marvel unmakes time, that here
Dread measures the brink of the gulf,
And does not shrink,
Love sees how vilely it must live,
And smiles?

V

DEPARTURE

The sensual parade of summer thins.
Green music, humming thighs, keen tambourines
Fade into grass. Crossing the dusty road,
Who hears the tune the caterpillar sings?
Noon's blaze has shrunken. Cool as lemon skins
The light that meadows wash their faces in.
Leafage crowds close, but richest boughs bear stains
Of tired banners, sunken. Lakes and winds
No longer leap in recognition, only
Begin to speak, and then are dumb again.
This opulence is tarnished. It is known
A shining fortune waits the season's heir,
But what was wealth is spent. This is the ebb
Of glory. How things end. When dark puts on
A widow's mournful jewel, say, the moon.

THE LOTUS

Steps in the tomb, uneager visitors,
Cannot
Disturb the flower of silence.
So the chill
Museum air can never hurt this bloom.
What if a sepal's blurred,
Not in a year, not in five thousand years
Was one leaf shaken from
That still stone flame. Let come
A hasty embarrassed boy,
Or some strange embarrassing lady, come and depart,
The silence does not change; their eyes, their fingers
Have not disturbed the flower.
The heart of stillness knows
An answering heart.
The master of the house
That is his tomb, the crowned king, silently
Receives the offerings in silence made.
Men bring him drink, bring jars of beer and wine,
They bring him food, vegetables, bread, meat, fruit,
And bring
Bowls, look, of lotus flowers.
Stone without fragrance,
Figures of the dead:
Can these have power
As wine and meat, as beer and bread? And yet
We eat and drink of them;
But chiefly on the lotus feast.
This is the flower of forgetfulness
To taste whose breath
Is to be fed by the divine memory.
It is the flower
Of risen life, no tomb can keep.

A sage once said the mind of God forgets
Evil that men remember having done, as it remembers
The good that men do and forget.
Then were the mind of God even as the lotus, sweet,
Alive and tall.
Step from the tomb.
Step out into the daylight falling
On the street.
Leave the still tomb behind the soft-hinged door.
Yet you shall sometimes find the lotus flowering
In the mortal mind's so narrow room.

IT IS THERE

These are the streets where we walked with war and childhood
Like our two shadows behind us, or
Before us like one shadow.
                                    River walks
Threaded by park rats, flanked by battleships,
Flickering of a grey tail on the bank,
Motionless hulls
Enormous under a dead grey sky.
Farther, the harbor and the miscolored waters
Rocking their flotsam under the blank round eye
At the masthead staring down the rats to come,
Beyond the fisher gulls.
And the windows full of ropes and hardware,
Doorways, barreled, yawning on the dark,
Wall-eyed alleys, coils of husky smells,
The breath of journeys strong there.
Streets whose sordid beauty
                                    joked readily with hope.
The taller avenues,
And walls that smiled like unpurchased horizons,
Swung intimate views out of a foreign room,
Hung a gate upon a garden's fable,
Walls that frowned
With aged remorseless eyes
Or the gloom of thunderlit landscapes, opening
A door into that placeless country
Where the sad animal is blithe, free and at home.
Too, those halls
Where we stepped lightly among the creatures
Whom death had tamed, who yet crouched, sprang, or flew,
Fierce as hunger, graceful as joy,
Until we knew, as in a half silvered mirror, the half

Captive image of immortality.
These are the old places, and walking there
As then with war and childhood,
I look into the shadows' faces.
They appal.
              Yet often I will see
(The marvels floating alive upon that stream,
The breathing of delight like purest air)
Another place: that you contrived
Between midnight and morning
In your dream, and in the morning
Took me there.
              We greeted it, who could not stay.
But it is there,
Surviving disbelief, surviving even what the malign
    years prepare.

AN AUTUMN POEM

The air rich and thin; the colorless color
Of pasture bristles softly as feathers of fur.
But the wild is still.
                    Stubble is queens in homespun,
Their spiky crowns held higher than they were   ˙
Before their jewels went and they were drained of gold.
Now trees are flushed with wonder of leave-taking,
While the mild skies look on,
                        keeping a flock
Of birds afloat, like a scarf dreaming and waking.
Once more the genius of autumn,
                            how mutely, enfolds
A spent world, being ignorant of what spoke
In that thunderflash when all the dead
And all the living mingled in one smoke.

NIKÉ AT THE METROPOLITAN

Great-winged, as thirstily as an athlete you
Lean your headless throat upon the wind.
Your blind breasts
Remember how they once frowned down the sea.
But the prow
That outfaced Ptolemy is now worn stone,
And here is worse—
A plaster image of that faceless thing.
It is this age's curse
To look at you, goddess of Samothrace, and think,
No cause is just.
Yet, with shorn arms you nurse
Whatever infant triumph men will bring
To rest in your opposing thrust.

EXODUS 1947

'Twas just as dawn rose o'er the salt sea,
Close at anchor lay a ship to get them free,
She lay in the harbor lonesome alone,
And each soul aboard was alone.

She lay there loaded down with the Jews
Hell hadn't swallowed so the earth must now refuse,
But they still had the salt sea lonesome alone,
As each soul on board was alone.

The ship was the *EXODUS 1947*,
Those aboard her ate a bread not made with leaven,
'Twas the bread of affliction lonesome alone,
They ate it with salt tears alone.

They made for Palestine across the salt sea,
Home they stole to their own country,
For there they'd not be so lonesome alone,
Oh, there they'd not be all alone.

The men on the *EXODUS 1947*
Asked if life could be recovered by replevin,
But the answer it left them lonesome alone,
Each man aboard was alone.

The women on the *EXODUS 1947*
Hushed the children with the name of Mr. Bevin
As they crowded together lonesome alone,
The big and the small, each alone.

Their mouths were parched, their hearts they were
    sore,
None to say it, they had known it all before

When they lay in the prison camps lonesome alone,
They lay in the camps all alone.

They sailed and sailed along the salt track,
Land of Promise sighted, there they turned them
    back,
Back where they came from lonesome alone,
No home save the salt sea alone.

Oh, what will they do and where can they go,
Back, turned back to the prisons of the foe?
For no country remains to the lonesome alone,
No place but the prisons alone.

There is one place that will not refuse
Some few thousand since it took six million Jews,
They may go without passport lonesome alone
And rest in the grave all alone.

Oh, let another dawn rise o'er the salt sea,
Let Death not be the Moses who will set them free,
But may all Pharaohs perish lonesome alone,
And no child be left all alone.

August 22, 1947

THE LOOK

Beneath the gay bandeau the shaven head
Showed. The eyes, huger in the wasted face,
Wandered like wild things dulled by narrow pacing.
The hand was tethered to a pain, that fed
On a spreading horror. Light revived the pain,
Reminding it how it had gorged before;
While off the brightness of the corridor
Some rooms were dark now where the dead had lain.
Talk fluttered heavily toward the neighbor bed,
In vain, moved toward the pain again, then tried
Circling some public topic, turned and eyed
The heart's homeliest charges, stiffened, fled.
The living stood beside the bed and waited
For nothing in the nowhere of appal,
And smiled at her, as if there were no wall
Between them and the dying. Her fate
Stood near them with eyes larger than her own,
That would not close, not even when she slept.
Its look followed after as they lightly crept
Off, waving, leaving her alone.

SCENE WITH FIGURE

The treadmill prisoner of that century
Whose sufferings seem quaint beside our own
Ground corn, ground stone. With steady tramping, she,
Repeating her grey round, grinds misery.
A choking heap, that she must eat alone.
Awake, asleep, she walks, she walks, she treads
The steps her crippled feet have worn. The crime
She pays for is a secret learned heads
Have not deciphered. But the few tears she sheds
Are salt as blood. Her heart burns like lime,
Destroying shriveled joy's long raveled threads.
She watches now the dying of her child
Whose life was empty as statistics are,
And all its broken furniture is piled
Beside her treadmill. This place is not wild.
It is a known spot on an unknown star.

VISIT TO THE ZOO

From great this, like that : the dust
Hissing beneath the bed,
The silence of all the dead,
From the abyss,
The fat,
We escaped to the hoofed and horned.

The rhinoceros's armature,
The rodent's play, the improbable
Giraffe was our delight.
The hippopotamus baby,
Solid, slow, and wide-mouthed as a dredge, showed the
    delicate
Pinkish grey of a young sunset cloud.
The crested curassow
Wore his huge sapphire as a prince
His caste mark, and the camel bore his hunch
As brother to the dunes.

We stood and stared
At the uncaring eyes of a sphinx-bodied cat.
Egypt sat in his pose who would not stir
More than a pharaoh throned, or
Couchant there, as if he were the form and pressure of
    the waste.
There was another whose gold thinly
Gleamed in his eyes alone, the rest was black:
So might twin moons ride implacable night.
And one, the ebony-striped, the sulphur-jowled,
Seemed the familiar of a rishi come
Down softly from his savage mountain home.
Farther, an infant dragon, neither tame
Nor yet breathing flame,
Perched the little leonine marmoset.

Reality was larger than the dream.
Eden so near a change,
The peacock's vulgar scream was consolation for
The splendor of his tail.
Translated fabulously from the Orient, from southern
    opulence,
Jungle, peak, plain,
Like living myths the creatures ranged
Across a landscape framed by skycrapers and tenements.
Not half at home, they were no stranger
Than those beseeching them for inklings of
Their kingdoms
And their power
And their glory.
Speechlessly, we too, laughing a little, with what love,
    what pain,
Told them our story.

DEATH OF A DOG

The loping in the darkness, here, now there,
As the wild scents whispered, the roadside beckoned, while
Things without heads roared past, their smell not vile
But meaningless—and the loping on, to where
A richer odor sang out like a snare.

Across the road it sang again, too strong
To leave, although a small monster was hooting
Behind, spoiling the scent, and suddenly shooting
Ahead, in a heavy stench, a wrench, a wrong
Noise of everything where it could not belong.

He got free, though, and with a limping leap
Found the high grass and panted there, his eyes
Twin frightened fires. He did not try to rise.
One leg was smutched, with oil, for the blood, deep
In the unscarred body, crept, then poured toward sleep.

He would have voided the strangeness: could not; strained
His neck toward some loosening of agony,
But could not reach it; grinning dreadfully,
Would have turned from the hand that stroked him and
    refrained,
But could not: could not stir. The hurt remained.

The hurt remained, the hurt, and the amaze,
As the eyes waned, like pin-point stars gone out
When darkness clouds. And now there was no doubt:
The leaping, the listening, the kind queer scent-crammed
    days
Were done. A dog's death is a death men do not praise.

HOMAGE TO PAUL KLEE

Itiskit, itasket,
A green and yellow basket,
                  green, yellow, brown, black,
I wrote a letter to my love
And on the way I
           lost
                it
(Will you ever get it back? Never never ask it).
But you know what was in it?

A mouse's minute.
A spicule's dream, a spider's whisper,
Fly's reply.
The twinkle in a needle's eye.
Tickle of a comet's whisker.

It can't be traced?
No land, no sea, no place, no face?
Once upon a space a town on stilts, a box in a box,
Sticks, ships, docks, locks.
No face. Giant cheeks.
No place. Fins and beaks.
      Arrows know where to go
      And they tell
      Radicle and pedicle.
No face, no place, no land, no sea,
But gastropod's geometry.
You hear if you listen well
           <   ^   −
Staccato : Crescendo : Forzando : Marcato :
               ∩
      FERMATA.

An echo after silence knocks.

FOUNTAIN AND UNICORN

The streets that offer it a snag-toothed smile,
An age that's paved with excrement, with wrongs
That choke the breath, could make the precious vile
If they could reach it, but how should they spoil
What to no street and to no time belongs,
Though it alight here for a bird-foot while?

Yet most securely housed, certainly wrought
In a given age are the proud things that tell
Less of the sweat spent on them and the thought
Or of the princely figure that they brought
Than they tell gaily like an astonished bell
The marvel that their imaging has caught.

For in a fountain, in a tapestry,
Saved from another time, paid for perhaps
With miners' or with ploughmen's agony,
And placed now for the whispering world to see,
To praise, to pass, look! there's a finger maps
The very heaven we dreamed could never be.

Beyond a portico presided over
By an angel, young, demure, with slotted wings,
The fountain, central, reigns. Thunders discover
A dewy dazzle, a mercurial hover.
Firm, amidst rushing joys, the fountain springs,
Sheds thunders, lifts the tower of a lover.

Tapestry shows the fabulous unicorn,
The gentlest beast that ever laid its head
Upon a lady's lap; like a tall thorn,
There both to serve the rose and to adorn,
Rises within her hand, which without dread
Clasps the white wonder, that resplendent horn.

These images are so noble they can call
Into the mind a thought that's fugitive
Yet noble, like themselves: instants where all
Speaks of supreme delight are radical,
There in the midst of death we live, we live
Where exaltation is most natural.

THUNDERSTORM, RIVERSIDE DRIVE

Who, above, prepares an austere fiesta?
None. It is carpets of cloud unrolling prove
The heavens desire dancing. Clearly they also
Require grey, for all wear grey. In an enormous
Hush the ethereal crowd advances.
It will have trumpets, drums. Are gay girls hidden
In veils O grey as fear? Are hierophants
Proudly pavanning toward a sacred murder?
Clouds
Are darkening here, nothing but clouds.

It is a huge fiesta, if austere:
Faces shrouded, feet shod with fog,
What appeared as gods or girls are mountains dancing.
Muffled their Highnesses are, yet moving lightly
As mist, they advance and bow, they retreat, they
    have changed
Places. It is a dance O it is a dance. Fire
Veins their approaching embrace. Have they kissed
At last, who vastly glow, part sombrely, go off?
Clouds
Are lightening here, nothing but clouds.

It is a fierce fiesta, no more austere
Than if clumped torches rearing on the rumps of
Elephants lit up an emperor's games.
The elephants trumpeting, the amphitheatre
Reverts O to a jungle clearing. About the kill
Fiery lions, ripping their feast, tread,
Bound and roar, grumble, roar, are still. The air,
Fanned with sound, cools.
Clouds
Are tumbling here, nothing but clouds.

The clouds roll forward greyly bellying. Rain
Pours down the cliffs, on the bunched factory lights
That quench and flare. Under fresh sluice the river is
Dimpling iron, and the beetlebacked limousines, like
    the asphalt, black
And bright. The thunder has stopped. The lurid branches
Of lightning, the hushed heat lightnings blotted out
By clouds loosing the rain. They pass away.
The rain ceases. There is nothing here
But memory of an austere fiesta.

LETTER TO WALLACE STEVENS

A man who looks at New Haven, with autumn ruddy
As never before, blue as never before,
Dawning on body and mind, you talk to yourself
Of auroras: we are allowed to overhear.
The core of it all is autumn—harvest in kind:
The senses admiring the delicious drench
Of light, of color, of texture, taste, and sound,
Fruit, flower, sail in the sun, a woman's hand,
Her voice, slight and abounding instruments.
Quench these, there's more: the mind, this instant holding
The manifold remembered, the intended
Huge imaginings. Now. Here. And next year or tomorrow
Where? The core of it is autumn, winter's dawn.
But no fear of the pathetic leave-takings
Known to branches above New Haven streets,
Nor the rude soliloquy on beaches smitten
By an easterly wind. Say, *heavy, heavy,*
Hangs over your head, as in the children's game.
The forfeit is heavy, but your talk is light.
Thirty-five years we have known your tinka-tonk,
Azay and rub-a-dub. This is not new
But it is not the same. Your lunar blue
Spangled with ambiguities, your roses
And crow's feathers are viewed under a cloud
And yet they shine in the eye. Now when you speak
Of dirt and dilapidation it is at once
As one of many and as a man alone.
But you are not solemn with Necessity,
The goddess as step-mother. You invite her in,
Into a room shining with mirrors, large,
Windowed to entertain the sun and moon.
She looks at herself in your mirrors, you at her.
You talk to her like a philosopher

But the eschatology, the entelechies,
  Are framed in your little language, with *musica*
  And *Gemütlichkeit, accent aigu ou grave.*
  You are no less a sensualist for being
  A voluptuary of the mind. But whether you hum,
  Or drum on the table, or try to sum it all up
  In words, French, German, Spanish, and your own
  Inventions, it is the pulse of autumn beating
  Under it that we hear. You make us see
  More than the golden boughs and the sky, cold,
  And blue as flame, to the smell of burning trash.
  You mention ferns and we suppose a pun
  Upon *die Ferne,* the famed for being far.
  For you fern-green, leaf-green, ice-green, are equal.
  For you in the night, off in the arctic, rosy
  As your bouquet, Aurora borealis
  Glows for the giant's table. Put
  These images aside. Let us say simply
  That a good poet in an evil time
  Speaks of the beginning of the end.
  He speaks of autumn, that's the dawn of dying.
  He speaks of the fact, the event, the thing and the
        thought,
  Trying to hold what's final in his mind.
  Thanks, Wallace Stevens, for what you say,
  And the way you say it and sing it, grave and gay.
  Whether the early morning makes you brave
  Or the colors of autumn delight you, clearly you have
  The courage of a plumbed ignorance. Your words
  Reveal an unrivaled joy to which death is
  Irrelevant. You give us the fiction and
  The festive real. They dance against the sky,
  Blue, burning, of your New Haven autumn,
  And we salute them, crying good-bye, good-bye.

HOMAGE TO JOHN SKELTON

Your name is Parrot: "a bird of Paradise"?
In Heaven, they say, Hebrew is the Word,
While you use every language, naughty or nice,
Greek, Latin, Welsh as you were Dylan's bird,
Italian, Castilian—good Skelton you've skirred
Hither thither hardily, but, spoken or sung,
Harsh or silk-soft, yours is the English tongue.

It was not made in heaven: the marriage of French
And Anglo-Saxon that bred this mongrel thing.
Is it spoken in hell? It could sweeten that stench.
Yet, Skelton, no skald had such black words to bring
Down thunders: your angry English would fling
Foundations asunder, you cared not who was bruised,
Cardinal or king, so truth was not abused.

Men envy young Tudor, Henry the Eighth,
Not venery's prowess in chamber or wood,
Nor finesse on the flute, nor his ownwayish faith.
It is this Tudor's tutor they'd have if they could:
John Skelton—what pedagogue stands where he stood?
Learned laureate, wit without peer,
He rhymes you as fast as a sailor will swear.

When Henry was England, that tongue was not still:
You mocking Parrot, up on your perch,
You plucked out false feathers with a bold bill,
Charged churchman and challenged church,
Keen to scour what scoundrels would smirch.
And priest that you were, you were handsomely human,
Who named as your wife your lifelong woman.

Psittacus, papagei, periquito, say
Your paternoster, greet us in Greek,
Coo like cocksparrow, jar like a jay,
Sol-fa like a lark, follow your freak—
Your voice is our joy, if you sing, if you speak.
A more than four centuries' marvel, in truth
Are you parrot or phoenix, of unquenchable youth?

Verily, perroquet,
Your vivacious play
Should not a whit dismay
Maître Mallarmé.
Both sagacious birds,
You both made poems with words.
You had only to call,
The words came, one and all,
The tiny words, the tall,
The fragrant, the fresh
As a fine peach's flesh
Or silken purse's mesh.
Nor you did not disdain
The shaggy words, the plain
And nasty, as though they'd lain
Nightlong out in the rain.
You used both smooth and rough,
Choosing the proper stuff
And not more than enough.
Your Elinour Rumming
Has our ears humming.
Our eyes are dizzy,
Our stomachs queazy,
Only to be thinking
Of her and her drinking,
She pouring it out
For bout after bout,
But you made us dafter
When you came after
To pour us a draught, half grief, half laughter.

Our hearts you still harrow
For Jane Scrope's poor sparrow,
Was killed at Carowe
By Gib the cat.
We are sorry for that.
And though again
We may laugh at Jane,
We are fond of Jane
And feel her pain.
You made poems with words
Like all sagacious birds.
And if your rhythms go tumbling,
Bumbling and rumbling,
So that some grumble,
Declaring you fumble,
Then their wits are numb
As a frostbitten thumb
That can pick up no crumb.

Though not few commend you, the fewest command
Your turn of the tongue. Those rhymes proffer choice
Of the spicy, the bitter, the fragrantly bland.
We breathe the fresh whiff of your verse, and rejoice
In Parrot's rich colours, his various voice.
Tutor us, John Skelton, who whetted your beak
On the bars of your cage; tell us how to speak.

Teach us to sing truly as you did, whose words
Would first prick the proud, then beguile a young child.
Throats of another feather yearn over the turds
In this age; too, cages are differently styled.
This bird's locked in the language, the other is exiled.
You seized liberty. Is it out of our reach
Who labor to arrive at your natural speech
For our gardens, our graves, for the tower, for the dive?
While your lessons flourish, English is alive.

BALLADE FOR BRAQUE

Though all's in pieces, how it holds.
Though all is flat, how still the eye
Goes round and round until it molds
The lifeless lines to something wry
But motionable, that must fly
Or fall, the mind rejoicing in
Deceivers we cannot deny:
Apples, cards, and a mandolin.

This is our world. Without the golds
Spilled heavenwise out of the sky
On valleys, pavements, waters, wolds.
Without the darkness we defy
Night after night. Skew shapes that cry
With voiceless lips and lipless grin
Can yet delight us, so we try
Apples, cards, and a mandolin.

Here are such simple manifolds,
Order so chanced it seems a lie,
No heartfelt warmth, no thrilling colds—
Collage like sherry, pale and dry.
Why does it tell us we shall die?
Or is it here that we begin,
Playing with things that say good-by:
Apples, cards, and a mandolin?

Painter, your abstracts magnify
What is not shown. We are Adam's kin
And we must pluck, not knowing why,
Apples, cards, and a mandolin.

"ENTERTAINMENT IN THE PARLOR AT 8:30"

The restless ones are small,
All eyes and knees.
Unable to recall a time not this,
They peer, they climb and crawl;
Their cheeks like fruit, their daring
Spicy with fear. But soon—never—but soon
Their joy must jump the moon.
They sigh: to draw a deeper breath
Would be to draw a knife.
What do they hope for?
O magician, come!

These sit along the aisles
On folding-chairs
Planted as firmly as their white-cheeked smiles
And ladylike white hair.
They seem at peace; they are wearing
Old pains in secret, like old-fashioned styles
In underthings. What creaks
Is not their patience. If they speak,
It is below the breath.
What do they wait for?
O magician, come!

FEEDING THE CHICKENS

Yellow yellow yellow: you are the child's
First richness, piled in a cornbin's hillocks.
Farmer gives her a fistful, hard to hold.
Of the crammed kernels, a few spill.
Hard to lose: the dribble of orange bright
Sunny white-tipped seeds. Two all but golden
Chips burst through the tighter clutch. Farmer
Seems not to mind, but so much beholden, the small girl
Wonders. And she may carry the crowding yellow
Handful out to the yard? Among queer feathered smells,
Craned pecking necks, and she may call
"Here chick! here chick!" and they will come?
And she must throw the sunny grains to them,
Yes: from the farmer's pan take more and more to scatter
Wide as she can, spattering a yellow hail.
Funnily they run to find it, greedily fight
To pick it up; bested by the stout fellow with the
     proud crest,
They bicker, cluck and peck. "Here chick, here chick!" But
Soon, too soon it's gone: among the gravel,
Droppings, feathers, the prodigal wealth dispersed,
     snatched up
And swallowed. The small girl, abruptly bereft
Of glory, is left empty-handed.
Farmer's leathery face turns toward the barn, his other
     chores.
She will go and play. Not now, but right away. Here
     still the spell
Of the warm brightness that she held so tight
Hovers: yellow yellow yellow

JULY IN DUTCHESS COUNTY

It glides and glints,
A straw bead picked out by the sun:
One bird note.
A green wind
Blows in the morning,
Dozes at noon, turns
Over, lazily
Ruffling a hay-colored warmth.
Late, the dry
Timbal of the cicada,
Like the pledge of the knifegrinder's wheel,
Refines
Summer's declining edge.

PORTRAIT

The bird's nest, empty, on her table, feeds her,
Far from a Chinese chowder of gummy nests.
She has so small a body, she finds a feast
In a slenderer soup, or in its fragrances.
Someone absconded with her childhood; early
She learned to wipe the fingers of her mind
Like the Prioress at meat. But a tiger paces
Her nights. In the grassy morning she chases the cat
From a wee bit rabbit, it limps off, she is bleeding.
And mends her wounds, and would admire the tiger
For its barbarous grace. She keeps a map of the tropics
A puritan ancestress left, and her garnet from Etna,
Entertaining eternity with a scrap of chill fire.
It is Sunday; the chromium twinkles ironically
In the room, while her love moves round a ghostly branch
That beckons backward, the torn wood gesturing still:
A wave, arrested. For the girl remembers
Years when the dry past was her dancing partner;
The stalk, the straw, the rain of Hokusai
She salutes: in field or sky, whatever is drily smiling.
But the deserts do not tempt: a single sand
Is her sufficient Sphinx. And she may hear it
Sing, she thinks, as the sun, rising, strikes.
But now she is moving into a nearer music,
That visits her pillow at midnight, after the padding
Of the tiger goes off, and the terror, although she knows
Fear of a sort, as she listens. And the night is soft.
She trembles, remembering as she forgets, asking
If the voice in her veins dissembles. It is sweet
As before, rough as never before. She hears famished crying,
Yet under and over it, wordless, like the world,
A song that is too human for a bird.

THREE NUNS LISTENING TO CHOPIN

Stiff as buckram,
Swathed in black and white
Strict as the keyboard,
Three tall ladies lean
Forward—confessing distance
Or delight?

The first phrase
Sparkles like the invisible spire
Fountains exhale, O the first notes
Adorn the air.
Surprising as a child's laugh rising
Higher, higher, higher, the chimes
Must drop—or stop.

Slow, melody climbs again,
Naturally, as a vine grows,
As though the fingers on the piano
Put forth
Buds of sound.
They, too, dewily sparkle.
But, sisters, do you hear
How soon the blithe tones darken, as leaves do,
And their afternoon
Shadows?
Can you recall,
Sisters, the grieving of desire?
Do you fear the advancing shade?
Pray, what shall you do who cannot do
What the piano does when rightly touched?
Even while it smiles, the music
Twinkles like a tear.

As years, years ago for the composer,
Now it is over
For the hearers, for the musician
Drenched in rosy thunders of applause.
She bows
To you, sisters, to all,
As when she leaned above the keyboard she
Bowed to the laws
Governing a strict love.

PARADIGM

Firm as young bones, fine as blown spume, still
As recognition.
The tree holds itself
In air, in winter. It looks imaginary.
Yet is earthfast above the shelf, what's drowned
Is bound to the rooted tree by moonlight only.
No starer at its own ghost, no creature
Lost in belief and terror is standing there.
Stilly, a tree greets a tree equally
Still. It shares, or they grown one
Share the old elements: water, earth, air,
In ashwhite body and hair memory of fire.
And yet the tree and its light image look
Like nothing that our planet bears. They are those
Who know what men do not. The force of anguish,
Of delight, bite of ambition, are human, are not theirs.
They are set apart, and solitary, together
Plunged in pale night. They have no will
But recognition.
This is their only meaning.
Tree, tree in the darkness
Of air, of water. Still. And alone.

THEY CAME TO THE WEDDING

Like gods who are fêted,
Like friendly old slaves,
Their silence full of music,
Their hands full of flowers,
Singly, in waves,
They came to the wedding.

First, sceptred with sunlight,
Slicing the shadows,
The Pharaoh came decked
In power, in sereneness
Like that of the lotus,
The lively, erect
Flower of forever.

The empress of China
Paraded her dragons
Of silver and gold,
While mountains were unloosing
Their hair to the music
Waterfalls trolled
Like bells for the wedding.

Saints came and sailors
With stories of marvels
And marvellous gifts,
And masts that now were branches
Broke into bird-song
Floating in drifts
Down branching horizons.

The deserts danced after,
The rivers before,
Till darkness like a mortal
Denying immortals
Thrust from the door
Those who came for the wedding.

DESIGN

These part us, if at heart we are embraced,
Their savage silence admits no reply:
Mountains of miles, the waters, and the waste.

As hungry fasts are haunted by the taste
Of festivals gone by, the days go by.
These part us, if at heart we are embraced.

We have admired together vases chased
With peak and cataract; now stretched eyes deny
Mountains of miles, the waters, and the waste.

Familiar streets, intimate rooms, erased
By them, revive, but soon our minds let die.
These part us. If at heart we are embraced?

Fresh pleasures glow, old troubles are outfaced
By stranger troubles, all nothing, against those high
Mountains of miles, the waters, and the waste.

The punishment for lovers who have disgraced
Love, so divided, we begin to try.
These part us, if at heart we are embraced:
Mountains of miles, the waters, *and the waste.*

DESTRUCTION OF LETTERS

To shred them: a narrow labor, and simply toss
The pieces away like peelings. Fingers tear
The heavier sheets across, across, across,
In voluptuous bravery; so children pare
Skin from a wound half-healed, admiring loss.

A phrase, like a deep look, glows from this pale
Manila paper: now flurrying, as past clutch
As confetti for the street sweeper to nail.
The word that a moment since was to behold, to touch,
Collapses into an impalpable Braille.

Postcards resist squarely, stiff to defeat
The redoubled twitch would slice them like a knife;
As if each public view—park, river, or street—
Were alive and clinging to its private life:
All that the eyes have loved returning in retreat.

What's left then? Mincings like receipted bills.
Those lines where the ink throbbed like an artery,
So littled, would not serve a fire by way of spills.
Yet in the widowing wrist the pulse more stubbornly
Beats: the heart swears: memory salutes, and kills.

LANDSCAPE WITH FIGURES

Granite-beaked, this dense green-feathered shore
That the world bangs beyond.
Shadows on the lake
The wind
Brushes to colder lustre.
Plumes, rocks,
Are shaped to echo stillness alone.
That cradling sound, that plop of hooves drops from
No hoof: is chestnut-colored water lapping stone.
Those granite beaks will stoop only
To feed, like father eagles, the dusk hush,
The sky before sunrise, the lonely light
After the sun has left heaven and lake both bare,
What do they hear but the pure music of
Silence?
Those multitudes of stars with their blind eyes,
What beauty could they see
But solitude's?

PIANO RECITAL

(for Maro Ajemian)

Her drooping wrist, her arm
Move as a swan should move,
First singing when death dawns
Upon the plumaged flesh.
But here no swan wings thresh,
No river runs. A woman
Strikes hidden strings in love.

Now slow—as fronds of palms—
Her fingers on the keys.
Lifted, her listening arms
Ponder the theme afresh,
Until it seems young flesh
Is momently transmuted
To echo's effigy.

No no—the risen hands
Pounce on the keys, destroy
The hush, rush on, command
The blacks, the ivories,
In flight now with the keys
To grief's unwindowed prison,
To the low gate of joy.

She leans with sparkling looks
Toward the dark wood, her strong
Hands work as gleaners should.
Then, as who would caress
A birdlike wordlessness,
She stoops—to drink the meaning
At the still brink of song.

OCTOBER NIGHT

Declared, not like a child or an animal,
But with the clarity of a dead face,
The moon over the mountains. The dead dispense
Such indifferent radiance
On the dark; their smiling would appal.

Coops, barns, are shut, now there is none
In the fields. No spoor of what went galloping over
    the heavens
With the roar of fire. Poverty
Possesses the hills, the sky. Forgotten the glory
Of that hour when dying and living were one.

The All has shed the moon like a nail-paring.
Naked, it has night for its mirror, there
We may watch it, moving beyond us, to what bed?
If it spoke, who could interpret what was said?
If it slept, who would lay by the strange clothes it
    was wearing?

DIALOGUE

Deep night. I lay on my bed,
Only less alone than the dead
Because I had speech with my heart.
"Everything is refused!"
It was crying. I, disabused,
Replied: "We do not part."

Droning consumedly,
Hidden planes plunged by,
Rousing the heart's hunger.
I offered: "The famished bite
On the used rinds of delight."
That filled the heart with anger.

"Everything is denied!"
It cried. Then I replied:
"Heart, I have your lament
And you have got my voice,
In which you may rejoice,
Perhaps, when all is spent."

My heart acknowledged this
With: "Sing. Sing of the kiss
Given on the deathbed."
"Death's living differently."
"The kiss!" it answered me,
Who was less alone than the dead.

FOR DYLAN THOMAS
ON THE DAY OF HIS DEATH

"Do not go gentle into that good night," you told
The old man. It was not gentle that you went,
You who were young. Nor gentle can be the lament
Raised for you, near the white bed where you died,
And raised in the wild wave-beaten countryside
Of your own Wales when it's known there, raised again
Wherever women who knew what your love meant
Or men who drank with you beyond content
Remember you. And raised, in a grief half anger and
    half pride,
By those, your fellows, to whom your voice in song
Belongs while ears are lent to it, and hearts
Lean, too. "Do not go gentle into that good night,"
Were almost the last words you spoke in verse.
And now the night has got you. We rehearse
Your admonition gravely, hearing laughter.
How else think of you, who at your gravest were dafter
Than all, and at your merriest, most grave?
What's left? As long as records last, your voice;
As long as speech sings, or song speaks, your songs;
And courage, in the huge dark, to rejoice
For the fountaining joys you knew in the living light.
These shine in the darkness where you must lie now.
Oh, is not that a lie? Dylan, good night.

November 9, 1953

HOMAGE TO THE PHILOSOPHER

(for A. N. Whitehead)

Some things persist by suffering change, others
Endure: the mountain endures, endures and is worn down,
    after ages is gone.
But nature, the philosopher tells his brothers,
Offers another fact for them to brood upon:
Eternal objects. Color is such a one.

"It haunts time like a spirit. It comes and goes.
But when it comes," he reminds them, "it is the same
Color."
        These are years when even a child knows
Endurance. And the famished face of a war with no name
Persists through change. Yet there is a godlike game

For us to play, here, now. The eternal objects are
Our counters. Let our board be the ground,
Planted or paved, or the sea or the sky. In particular
And passing forms—color, shape, sound
Surround us, physical, fantasied, lost, and found.

Eternal red, orange eternal too, yellow, green, blue,
Eternal violet. Play with them, share their estate, set
Them up in the mind like circles and squares, like notes
    remaining true
Whether absent or there. They will vanish, not die,
    even if you forget
Red, orange, yellow, green, eternal blue, eternal violet.

THE POEM

The painter of Dante's awful ferry-ride
Declared the world only a dictionary,
Words, words, whose separate meanings must go wide
Unless the visionary
Compose them, so his eyes are satisfied.

The saint from Africa called every thing
A word, the world being a poem by God,
Each evil tuned to make a splendor sing,
Ordered by God
With opposites that praise His fingering.

Was Delacroix a fool? Was Augustine?
The dictionary seems a poor appliance,
With venerable terms become obscene,
Too fertile science.
We try the poem, but what does it mean?

The rhymes are slant, of course, the rhythms free
Or sprung, the figures moving through the mind
Close as a caravan across country
Often unkind.
It is magnificent in its privacy.

And yet the words are there: fire, earth, ocean,
Sound, silence, odor, shape and shadow, fear,
Delight, animal, mineral, time, space, motion,
Lovely and queer:
The crystal's patience, the baboon's devotion.

The words are there; according to his powers,
The saint, the painter, gave the work a gloss,
Loving it. Anguish, as it scours, devours,
Discovering loss.
The logic of the poem is not ours.

VI

EARLINESS AT THE CAPE

The color of silence is the oyster's color
Between the lustres of deep night and dawn.
Earth turns to absence; the sole shape's the sleeping
Light—a mollusk of mist. Remote,
A sandspit hinges the valves of that soft monster
Yawning at Portugal. Alone wakeful, lanterns
Over a dark hull to eastward mark
The tough long pull, hidden, the killing
Work, hidden, to feed a hidden world.
Muteness is all. Even the greed of the gulls
Annulled, the hush of color everywhere
The hush of motion. This is the neap of the blood,
Of memory, thought, desire; if pain visits
Such placelessness, it has phantom feet.
What's physical is lost here in ignorance
Of its own being. That solitary boat,
Out fishing, is a black stroke on vacancy.
Night, deaf and dumb as something from the deeps,
Having swallowed whole bright yesterday, replete
With radiance, is gray as abstinence now.
But in this nothingness, a knife point: pleasure
Comes pricking; the hour's pallor, too, is bladed
Like a shell, and as it opens, cuts.

AFTERNOON WITH AN INFANT

So pink, diminutive, so mute an O,
This infant yawn: we laugh at it—
The human thing;
The little animal has shown it shares
Our habits, not our suffering.

Its mother holds the creature on her arm.
It stirs her smile once more, with a
Bit sneeze, whose small
Concussion is of an insect tambour's force,
Yet intimately natural.

Those who will never again answer us
Seem at this instant further off:
We know them gone
Because they are speechless? Because we'll not hear
Them sneeze, nor ever watch them yawn.

MIDSUMMER POEM

Hard as a man's in the vintage,
The feet of the sun are trampling
The meadows, pressing the fields. Silence
Dances. Fragrance blazes. Noonward
A fresh sweetness
                beats up from the deep heat.
Whitest clouds hugely
                  carve heaven out of the sky.
At a shadow's prick, one bird
                  arrows from covert, is lost
Among thicker boughs:
                fright's gift
To the festival of noon.
Brilliantly
        stillness renews the dance.
Perhaps the grave
Pines, late, in their darkening grove
Will interpret it.

SUSPENSION

Hiding his golden abdomen, the Spider of the sky was
    at rest,
Like an unmoved Mover, beyond the shafts of his web.
Three separate spans ran to the river
Spread below, smoothed, as by the Spider's craft.
The threads caught upon silence
As if, the spinnerets stanched, those waters ceased their
    flow.
Like the hairs of a headless harp
The golden, the silvered, hung, singing
Quiescence. No bird in the branches. They were bare,
Brown as the earth. Brown as a high cloud's brow
    that frowned
Rosily beside blithe cheeks trumpeting.
Where all was utterly still.
The spans fanned out, three spokes of a tireless wheel
That would go nowhere: unfinished forever.
It would not roll toward evening,
Nor turn toward winter. Yet the air was dusk,
The sky cold. The Spider, hidden,
Softly mantled himself in the heavens of Tiepolo.

SMALL COLORED BOY IN THE SUBWAY

A slight-boned animal, young. What jungle fruit
Droops with such grace as you in the subway corner
In your Saturday suit? Your eyes, wide
With would-be wakefulness, are dark as plums
That have the aubergine's lustre, but your skin,
Smooth as an egg, offers the gentler color
Of coffee in the bean. You are a morsel
So fine that you feed the eye as other things,
Sweet-fleshed, pamper the palate. Now you lean
Lightly against your mother, in the surrender
Of weariness still keeping dignity,
As if, a child, you honorably upheld
What was too heavy for a child to hold.
The luminous look is hidden; your eyes are
Lidded at last. You sleep. The bleak surround
Crowds you a little. Yet, even in sleep,
Without defense, darkly your grace proffers
The grave accusation of innocence.

JULY DAY

The afternoon sways like an elephant, wears
His smooth grey hide, displays his somnolent grace,
    weighing
The majesty of his ponderous pace against
The slyness twinkling in an innocent eye.
An infant born to the jungle, this afternoon
Elsewhere reached its mammoth magnificence,
Achieving the delicate play of a palace creature
With which it moves.
Moves, yet those giant limbs, the hours,
Scarcely seem to stir.
Prehensile as leisure, the pleasure triumphing here
In the procession of summer balances
The sun in hiding, the moon, hidden.
Before those grey knees sink
A gaiety like the glint of ivory slides
Lightly along the sky. This elephant afternoon
Winks at the glory of which it is part,
And bears itself with patience. Soon
It will be trumpeting.

BARGES ON THE HUDSON

Going up the river, or down, their tuneless look
Is of men grown poorer who, though ageing, wear
Some majesty of the commonplace. Old barges
Are cousin to those whom poverty becomes—
To late November, the north, nightfall, all the
Deprived whom increment of loss enlarges.
They have no faces, have no voices, even
Of their own selves no motion. Yet they move.
With what salt grace, with a dim pride of ocean
Uncompassable by a fussy tug,
Prim nurse that drags or nudges the old ones on.
They must borrow their colors from the river, mirror
The river's muddy silver, in dulled red echo
A sundown that beds in soot. Their freight, rusty,
Faded, cindery, is like the past
The charwoman deals with. Yesterday's business
They carry with the dignity of the blind.
By night the river is black, they are black's shadows
Passing. The unwrinkled stars dispute that darkness
Alone with a lantern on a one-eyed spar.

DISASTERS OF WAR : GOYA AT THE MUSEUM

Streets opening like wounds: Madrid's. The thresh
Of resistance ends before a tumbled wall;
    The coward and the cursing sprawl
    Brotherly, one white heap of flesh
    Char-mouthed and boneyard black.
A woman, dragged off, howls—a lively sack
Of loot. An infant, fallen on its back,
Scowls from the stones at the Herodian lark.
Light is the monster fattening on this dark.

If shadow takes cadavers for her chair,
Where fresh fires glare life lifts a wolfish snout.
    Bruised and abused by hope, the rout,
    Turning, is gunned across the square
    And scattered. Rope, knife, lead
Slice prayer short. A lolling head
Grins, as with toothache. Stubbornly, the dead
Thrust forward like a beggar's senseless claw.
What is scrawled there in acid? THIS I SAW.

Beyond the Madonnas and marbles, Goya's brute
Testament pits itself against the hush
    Of the blond halls, the urbane crush—
    Against the slat-eyed, the astute,
    Craning, against the guard, who yawns.
And pits itself in vain: this dark, these dawns,
Vomit of an old war, things the nightmare spawns
Are pictures at an exhibition. We
Look, having viewed too much, and cannot see.

DAMNATION

Hell is not far below,
Not black, not burning,
Nor even past returning:
You come and go.

You go and come
As in a mirror,
But hell is nearer,
And not so numb.

And when you go
You do not lose it,
Because you chose it—
As you know.

URBAN PASTORAL

More domestic than elegant, leaves and pigeons
Hedge the dazzle beyond. Green, dust,
A purple strutting, screen the river's march.
The walks are for pigeons and ladies
Like parched pigeons, avoiding the bench where a tramp
Rustily sleeps. The carriages in the park
Are babies' now; children make all the traffic.
Spring brightly traveling, summer half awake,
Here the afternoon city plays at being
A dream of summer's: gaiety in repose,
Lazily festive as poster holidays,
A dream. Crossed by the tramp, rousing.
On paths where sparrows edge to snatch the bread
Crumbed for the humbled pigeons, the holiday
Is broken and scattered. Yet a strong green still
Throngs the boughs; and the river, preened, goes twinkling
Past all these birds, on to the salt sea.

AT THE GREEN GROCER'S

I

Oranges beam
Sleekly as mandarins.
Their cheeks grained
As mellow leather is.
Spice, like a bloom, feathers
The thin tough skin.
Where, on a street gone dark,
Lit windows
Hole the night,
Their cosy gold is fellowed.
They could boast of cousins
In ancient Spain.
Spheres of rosy gold, little yellow
Worlds heaped here at
60¢ a Doz.—
Sweet juicy
Oranges.

II

i

Shapely as violins, the pears
Look down.
These, rose-freckled like a strawberry,
Those, with an autumn cheek of withered brown,
Alike, their hauteur.

Beside the leek, Wales' pride,
The small white onions shine
As meek as pearls.

And pumpkins plump as camel-humps,
And squash: tapering
Fingers of light
Noon turns them to bright as butter thumbs,
Wartily gesturing to the sun.

III

The eggplant does not make the gaudy show
Of pumpkins or pomegranates. Like the crow
Blackbird: the purple grackle, like the 'cello,
The eggplant's note is resonantly low.

It cannot, like the pineapple, display
A finial elegance; lacks the holiday
Grace of the grape. Yet this fruit is shaped
And burnished as those eggs ostriches lay.

Lying so close to the potato bin,
It seems too gorgeous for that distant kin.
Between cusped amethyst and tumbled tubers,
Choose? Sometimes the stained earth-apples win.

IV

A large whitecheeked old woman smiling:
The homely solidity, the beauty of
The cauliflower is vulgar and beguiling.

Cauliflower, branched broccoli above,
And leafy sprouts below, all grown to please,
What share have they in the quality of love?

Nothing on earth is unromantic as these
But turnip lumps. The cauliflower's white
Florets, broccoli's green, are coarse as frieze.

The kale is blowsy. New cabbage, curled tight
As an embryo, the red, purply as cheap stained glass,
Are commoners, too obvious to delight.

Yet even the festive, rare asparagus
Does not take the eye like the simplicity
Of this vegetable that its neighbors here surpass

In voluptuous curves, color, delicacy.
There is a quality better than beguiling
In the cauliflower's homely solidity,
Like a large, whitecheeked old woman, smiling.

V

You with your brush bound to your swelled foiled hand
Would understand, old painter, this upanddown upanddown
Reaching and climbing. The grim grocer toils
Over his chiming pyramids, cares

Only for custom.
Each hour despoils the contrived order, evening
Destroys the flesh. With morning
Opulence is freshly alive,
Sounding the sun's note.
Blunt shapes under drumtight skins,
Sharp hues, some sweet,
Their vibrancy repeats: here is a man's
Livelihood; food to be bought, eaten; goods
Belonging to vision least.
The end here is still life. Custom provides
For the eyes first. They feast. Their feast invites
Thirst and delighted hunger. All are satisfied.

UNEARTHLY TOY

The river was blowing scarves.
They waved to a cloud as it flew
Round the sun-shod hour,
Who stepped lightly as dew
From a glowing
Green to, aloft, a widening stream of windy blue.

If pigeons, if people, strolled
And preened, it was gesture enough
For a saraband.
One stone angel took off
From the steeple:
Stone, or a puff of smoke, or wing's unfeathering stuff.

When dazzling there dartled—what?
A thing: was it creature or sleight
Of magician's wrist
That shone scarlet in flight?
If it startled,
How it seduced the eye where it dove and swam the height!

In derelict levity
Pursuing its willowy tail,
It was all a fling
Of twin ribbons, the gale
In a chevy
Ferried hilariously, then left to float and trail.

Now dolphin, then shying clown
On ski jumps of sky or the bight
Of an azure guy;

A laugh dancing; a mite
That in flying blazed like a crown, it winked out of sight,
The runaway kite, in a somersault's twinkle. O lost
Undying demon of delight!

HEARD IN OLD AGE

(*for Robert Frost*)

That sweet fire in the veins, while everywhere
The Harpies' filth keeps raining down, the young
Make love, make war, make music: the common tongue
Of private wounds, of the outrage that they share,
Or sing in desperate mockery of despair.

Is there a song left, then, for aged voices?
They are worse than cracked: half throttled by the thumbs
Of hard self-knowledge. To the old, dawn comes
With ache of loss, with cold absence of choices.
What heart, waking to this, drumming assent, rejoices?

Traffic rousing, gulls' cries, or cock crow, score
The body's ignominy, the mind's delays;
Till the Enigma, in a wandering phrase,
Offers a strain never audible before:
Immense music beyond a closing door.

SEASCAPE

Assembling ways to glisten,
Immensity
Is fresh as paint, and friendly,
Like salt.
Until wind pleats it, the water
Spends mica's childish glitter.
At the end of the jetty, erect,
Domestic,
A herring gull
Is the finial on the newel.
He stares westward,
No more prospecting for dinner
Than a saint on his pillar.
Marking the tip of the cape, the lighthouse
Off there is the size of the gull,
Equally singular, equally white.
The hush that sparkles in the sun
Is noon.

THREE VIEWS OF MOUNT RAINIER

i

An ethereal mountain, or
A firm-sinewed cloud?

ii

After Krishna had left off
Playing with the milkmaids,
They gave their milk and cream
To ingenious angels,
Who made for the God this
Giant ice cream, softly, slowly
Dissolving upon the snowy dish of Itself.

iii

Immaculate birth
                    of
          floating
Majesty   on those
Northern skies.
Immense as nowhere,
That rootless
               repose.

BERKSHIRE AFTERNOON

Those hills are hives swollen with honey
From the trees, under whose boughs tranquilly walking
We listen for thunders of the dancing bees.
Hidden in such a hive, summer,
Served like a queen long enough,
Waits
To depart serenely like a queen.
The garden celebrates the marriage
Of radiance and silence,
Disturbed by
Nothing bigger than a hummingbird,
Or an old man's shy cough.

COMING OF AGE

PHI BETA KAPPA POEM, COLUMBIA UNIVERSITY, 1957

I

From that close cave, kicking away its riches,
Who, fighting toward air, who, crying, comes?
Coming, daring it, who abruptly pitches
Into a dazzle that chills, a gulf that drums?
This wet furled blindness with a naked breech is
Without hope or heart. Feet, fists, and toothless gums,
It is no one yet. Simply it works to seize
Kindness somewhere out of such rough mysteries.

And kindness arrives, as we know; we know this, too:
Invisibles, giants, the mysteries, multiplying,
As the child grows and changes, change. Some few,
Transformed by their names, that are queerly satisfying,
Seem not so awful, as if the name were a clue.
The mysteries do not answer, uncomplying.
Yet, knowledge enlarging knowledge of ignorance,
Round the sage's rose of joy, girl and boy still dance.

They hear the Song of the Senses, as it rises
Out of the air, from water, earth, and fire.
They dance into the Kingdoms of surprises,
Where, innocent of repugnance and desire,
The mineral endures; where the thrifty plant devises
What offspring, what society require;
Where the animal, thrilling with fear, or joy,
Shares the brief particular fate of girl and boy.

II

i

The ancients named the four:
Earth, water, fire, air,
Whose grace all things living in rivalry still share,
Whose enmity grows more
By us, who dare to ignore
Their favors everywhere.

ii

Earth is dirt, is flesh, is flower,
The sheaf, the vine, the bony boughs.
Here the fox holes; here, if a hawk tower,
The rabbit prostrates; bullocks browse,
And deer. Here are parks, trenches, sloughs.

Earth, cousin to the wandering Seven,
Plays foster-mother to her slave;
Still set apart from hell and heaven,
She gives him what so long she gave:
All countries, and a grave.

iii

Mantling the planet,
The viewless tissue
Heaven's tailors issue
An emperor
For the world's wedding:
The air, goes threading
To the heart's core.
Flame, too, would vanish
If air were dying.
Of all things flying

She is the nurse:
Bomber and arrow,
The kite, the sparrow,
All these are air-borne,
So sound is air-borne, song, cry, or curse,
And uttered verse.

iv

Water is clothed with terror, pouring
However purely from the cloud.
Do the seas sleep? The old flood, snoring,
Acting its dreadful dream aloud,
Now shapes the cities' shroud.
The whale's road and the carrier's, water
Cradles the iceberg, rocks the buoy-bells.
Hers is that foam-bright-breasted daughter
Who copulates with war. Still the Unknown compels
Beauty and horror, joined beneath the swells.

v

If the earth, or if water, or air,
    Are elements and essence
Of the days and the nights that we share
    With each so mighty Presence,
And if water, and earth, and air, too,
    Are all we are heir to,
There is one rages deeper, flies higher—
In the deeps, in the vault, in the veins, there is fire.

Through only five Doors the acknowledged come:
Bringers of food, or flowers. Accusers from
The Egypts and Israels of the soul pass there.
They admit a dark that dazzles, lights that numb.
Ocean's breath pours through those Doors; and stale
    smells crawl
Across the sills. Through them the madrigal,
The bloody noises come. They open on nothingness,
And it enhances that narrow room they wall.

      O beat, beat to the music
      Of every mortal sense,
      Heart; it ushers another
      As human, and more immense.
      Deaf neither to shrieks nor stillness,

      O dance when you can dance
      To that small music's prodigal
      Mortal resonance.

ii

Even a stench can speak comfortably:
The freshness of earth, warm with horse-droppings,
Clogged seines, reeking richly of the sea.
An herb, pinched, pleasures, but no less the stings
Of woodsmoke, benzoin, rosin, pitch; such things
Haunt like cherishing ghosts who try to tell
How much is brief and lifelong, like a smell.

iii

In his Great Summons the Chinese exile plied
His vacant soul with memories: of song,
Of beloved vistas, of the bright-lipped, bright-eyed,

Revels, high deeds; but first with subtle or strong
Meats, sauces, wines. Relish, time does not wrong,
The condemned approve. Sweet at the tonguetip, taste
Still keeps its sweet, if bitter at the last.

iv

Music is chief of savors, hot or cool;
It is sorrow's physic, that desire will greet
Gaily as nutriment. Music is a pool,
Where beasts from the wilderness of the spirit meet
To drink, then with jungle courtesy, retreat.
Noises pollute it; only stillness clears,
To make purer music for whoever hears.

v

Is vision deaf? Lofty waterfalls make wing
From the Zen master's brush as rhythm flows.
The Persian's orange, azures, crimsons, ching
Like a celesta. Suns' fanfare, arpeggios
Of rain, the planets' inscrutable pavan, these shows
Ring in the mind's ear as a look will. Sight
Has the key to the City of Knowing, and of night.

vi

Unravelling airs, the hackles frost-crisped turf
Erects; the crag that scorches like a nettle;
Silken brutality of assaulting surf;
Pure heat, and clawing cold; clay, marble, metal;
Knives; the finger that brushes like a petal:
All this touch knows, who knows the profoundest kiss,
And the utter pang that robs her of all this.

IV

i

Overwhelmed, deprivation shuffles:
Which goods shall it choose, ignore?
While from all regions, from all seasons,
The senses as before
Ask dues, that, if arriving, shrink and
Will soon arrive no more.

And though, blind trudge, the body shoulders
His fellow whom circumstance
Has lamed, will then the soul, as promised,
Be blessed with legs and prance?
A fable. Yet as the players are leaving,
O what a dance we dance!

ii

Lovers under the lamps dance or dream of dancing;
In smuttiness, in trash on the street the children's feet
Flash. At particular births perhaps a star will dance.
Swaddled in his mother, the infant kicks his heels,
As the heart of age, surprised, reels in death's pouch.

There are many musics. There is their absence, certain
As mischief: the routine disquiet, not just
Hysterical voices of traffic, static, kitchen noises,
But, repeated like crazy phrases, repeated invasions,
All those Times of Troubles that leave the gayest mind
Ignorant where, in the rubble, among the blind, the crippled,
The orphaned, the unburied, it may find some friend.

Ignorance is the Law. Created to sparkle,
A jewel or a snowflake: the crystal, flawless
As the mathematics of its symmetry,
Knows nothing of that multiplying marvel.
The cancer cell breeds, breeding in ignorance
Of what it havocs. The vulture in his eyrie,
Wolf in his lair, dolphin under the wave,
The rat in his clean cage, kills, is killed,
But, living, is ignorant that it must die.

Ignorance is the law, that men have broken,
To be punished: radiant science half confirms
Nebulous Genesis, and to be rewarded
Like rebels who find triumph is their fate.
The lights among which we move, pushing the darkness
Farther back, show it as darker now
Than the long northern night, and how immense,
Flourishing: an expanse of darkness,
As if the lights themselves were the nourishment
Darkness seized on, to grow. This monster, the creatures,
Alert to a whiff, a whisper, of the enemy,
To his shadow stirring, victims of beak, barb, snare,
Have never feared, have met nowhere. It is this monster,
That makes no sound, that has no shape, that must
Trivialize everything human, must also
Transfigure the trivial, making it most dear.

The ancient elements surround, support us:
The senses, while they can, sing their five songs,
Of everything, desired and undesired,
That belongs to being; alike the actual,
And the imagined, springing from that root
Like the golden Phallus that rises from the lake
At Mount Meru's foot, from which stream men and gods.
It is of common things the senses chiefly
Sing, or speak: of things that are palpable,

Things that address the nostrils or the tongue,
The usual scene, the ordinary sounds.
But silence is what echoes at nightfall.
Nor does that seem a supernatural voice,
Though it is as if the darkness found
Speech for such final greetings, such farewells
As strike the heart dumb—the ignorant heart,
That in despair first learns how to rejoice.

SPACE MAN

Jetted like the circus's
Human bullet, he'll face
A public privacy
For the space of his throttled jaunt.
Returning,
Will he be implacably displaced,
Haunted by earthlessness?
Craving the unknown, he endures,
Abides its brood of dangers,
Even this one of being
Always a stranger
To those riding at our planet's pace only around
The simple sun.

May, 1959

N.Y. TANKA

The nightboat moving
Down the river: legs of light
Twinkling, how quickly
That caterpillar glides off,
Trailing the still joyful dark.

SUMMER POEM

Rich heat of August sweetens
Young apples on the boughs
Beyond the resinous road.
Beyond turf's dapple, drowsing.
Cicadas bell the time
Of year, but no tale's told
Till the cool-throated tones
Of the church on the hill
Shadow their unstilled shrilling.
As in the hand of the wind,
The sprinkler's water-fan
Sways lightly over flowers.
Marigold, zinnia, lily,
Phlox, dark primulas
Burn in the nooning light.
Azure's immaculate
As candor here. A cloud
Mimics a cherub's flight.
The equinox seems near.
And peace awhile, mockingly
Lovely and grave, returns.

ADMONITION

The graveyard and the garden share
A streetlamp like a gibbous moon.
As crisp as frost, soft as a plume,
Its ghostliness invades the room:
The mirror beckons, shadows pale and stare.

No shape, however sharp, is true.
Darkness and hoar divide the scene.
From what will be, from what has been
Cut off, this world is wholly clean.
Washed in cool unreality like dew.

Vision absconds, as with the dying.
Now sound, if growing more, if less,
Sound, perfected in formlessness,
Possesses all. Blow, or caress,
What sound thus offers there is no denying.

Secret as silence, in the turf
Around the gravestones on the hill
As in a ripening orchard, still
Thin pulses quiver, wince, and thrill
Like the blind shrilling of a spectral surf.

Nothing can drown them but the voice
That issues from the bell tower's throat,
As *one*, and *two*, and *three*, the rote
Of those bronze resonances float,
Calling to wake, or sleep. Calling: "Rejoice!"

THE DISENCHANTED

The pointed savor of a pineapple,
A world of corners, each hiding surprise,
And melancholy, as in a giraffe's eyes:
The kingdom of childhood is dappled glory. Old,
We are like prisoners at their exercise.

Here nothing shines. Night passes. The bare street
Under that stone sky is Chirico's.
Shadows are cut by a grey light that glows
Like the cheek of a ghost. Mystery, once alive
With promises, now clings to what death knows.

Morning returns. Though snow is on the river,
The famous punctual daffodils return.
Young lovers lie together. They will learn
The truth that holds us still. Loss is our jokesmith,
And tenderness the fire with which we burn.

CÉZANNE

Air. Light. Energy. A birth of joy
As if this peasant earth, free of the embrace
Of an invisible god,
Not quite asleep, half smiled, remembering.
The mountain : here. The mountain : here. Always
The same, different in all ways. The mountain
Clearly rejoicing in the morning;
Smoldering in the moody afternoon;
No sadder than courage, the mountain shouldering
The soon familiar weight of dusk.
And once more earliness. The windy whites
Of a fresh day, blue that dares not, then dares.
The mountain's dream at dawn. The playful hush
That holds the saplings. The bare road turning
Into the woods. Still expectancy.
The green voice of the alleys triumphing
While it recedes. Powerful counterpoint : stark
Chill of cliffs; the wintry stream.
Stroke upon stroke, square upon square of white,
The loaded brush, the palette knife, five
Yellows, six reds, four blues, only three greens
Have ripened apples that spill into now, thrust up
A mountain's life. Paint giving the unseen
Shapes that cast shadows. Inscapes of delight. Silence,
Tumultuous or serene. Shadowless mystery.

LIZARD AT POMPEII

Little finger of fiery green, it
flickers over stone. Waits
in a weed's shadow.
Flashes emerald—
is gone.

Here once horror poured so hot, heavy, thick,
everyone was dead before he was sick.
Now here is no heat but the sun's
on old stone treads;
no motion but that rippling inch of whip:
yours, you little live jewel, who slipped away
into silence. Yet stay on to haunt memory,
like those dead.

A VIEW OF THE PIAZZA DI SAN MARCO

Shaking the glory of Heaven from his heels, perhaps an
    angel
fled to this earth, this Italy, these Venetian
lagoons. Where, in the hilarity of escape, he soon
designed a place to walk in: the piazza,
spacious as (knowing no other) Heaven's courts
        were spacious.
Beneath the bare azure it lay, as immensely empty.
The piazza was all that was there.

An angel, too, can be lonely.
But the runaway knew what to do: he sang
a Mozartean phrase that peopled the place with doves,
if emblems of Christ, sacred to Aphrodite. Yet the piazza,
for all the froufrou of their fluttering, their rou-cooing,
        glittered in sunshine:
empty still. He waited.
Something was wanting there beyond the birds.

And then he remarked the far end of the square.
So surely it was that San Marco sprang to life, winged
        and a lion
at play with a Byzantine empress, dazzling,
at the far end of the square.
Marble dreaming, mosaic blazing, triumphant bronze,
stone holding ivory's delicacy in derision,
spire on spire, dome smiling on golden dome, gonfalons
        streaming,
power, opulence, gaiety dancing together:
the vision of a truant angel.

Then the dark chime of the Moors' twin hammers
    resounded and
like a billow in spume dissolved, where refined planets
    spangled the azure, in the zodiac's golden circle;
and above it a lion couchant folded his wings
as if time were no more.
Almost a rebuke, on the right—the stern campanile.
Oh, but he needed more than the doves and the dazzle,
who felt a little the burden of his being
in Venice, on the Piazza di San Marco.
He paced the length and the breadth and again
    the length of the piazza, reflecting,
till out of his reflections—as palaces
in Venice rise out of the water—shadows arose,
and multiplying and petrifying and arching
elegantly, formed those lofty arcades
endless and grey as trade,
yet, with Venice glass iridescent as the necks of doves,
with Venice lace, as befits a city that is bride of the
    sea,
sumptuously graceful.
But the unearthly stranger, he did not know why,
    dissatisfied, shook his wings,
putting the doves to frightened flight, who alighted again
before the arcades, croodling and strutting and gleaming.

Then the angel knew what he must do. He sang
a second phrase, if less than Mozartean, festive
as a wedding. It was *Tischlein-deck-dich* on the piazza's
either flank. Parasols, yellow or red or blue or yellow,
    hugely sprouted
like mushrooms in a fairy ring; strings being stroked,
    plucked strings,
decanted music like a light wine, glasses were lifted like
    singing. Above,
a sky intensely azure. Beneath it, two or three children
    scattering

[163]

glistening grain to the doves; while at either side
    the piazza, men and women,
rosily aureoled, sat at their several tables, in a dream
of a Byzantine empress pavanning with a winged lion, with
    birds alighting and flying, with music sparkling like
    wine, and everyone
rejoicing in the grandly absurd pinnacled marvel,
    as in the piazza, immense
as the courts of Heaven.

And the soft and the savage voices of wounds were silent.
Soilure was washed away.
There was no shadow
But the slight shadows of the wings of doves, and the
    colored parasols' flanges.
As, in love,
joined pleasures, burning, kindle a universe,
here earth and Italy, Italy and Venice, Venice and her
    piazza fused, and from that central splendor shed
    such light
as, for an hour,
undoes the whole world's night.

THE MOTHER

On the hilltop, close to the house of the empress,
    Your temple
Is dark, sunken: a pit. The thick crowded pillars
Stumps only. The dread of Your presence
Lopped, like them, cold in mutilation.
Throning it here, in the stillness: vacancy.
In times beyond this time, were you robed in darkness?
You were known, then, as the Great Goddess. You are
Great even yet, more terrible, Mother Cybele, now you are
    nothing.

PASSAGE

It is their twittering that shimmers; it is their droning
That steadily hones the stillness. They remain hidden.
Invisibly, summer is passing. A flight not noticed
Like her warmth, her fragrance in passage,
Unless by these noises, that will be matched, at night,
By the brilliance, the sustained distance, of
        constellations.

LATE REFLECTIONS

Old and sick, you turn away from mirrors, whether
They show the mocking face years have stained and withered
Or reflection quails at the coward's mean gesture.
Images of body and soul. What is the soul?
A feather blown by odd weathers of shine, of shade.
And the body? Is shaper and shape of the soul.
Sick, the pair live by the clock in a placeless time.
Old, they live in a futureless place, where odors
And a few fragrances are lingering features.
Hard to remember, the shape before it was fixed
As it will be in death, and as hard to believe
The remembered was once pure possibility.
In our grandparents' days, not blind superstition
But the love that illumines reason required that,
After a death in the house, mirrors be covered.

FIREWORKS

Not guns, not thunder, but a flutter of clouded drums
That announce a fiesta: abruptly, fiery needles
Circumscribe on the night boundless chrysanthemums.
Softly, they break apart, they flake away, where
Darkness, on a svelte hiss, swallows them.
Delicate brilliance: a bellflower opens, fades,
In a sprinkle of falling stars.
Night absorbs them
With the sponge of her silence.

VOICES ON RIVERSIDE

in homage to WILLIAM CARLOS WILLIAMS

Vermilion. Orange. Two shirts
on two darkskinned boys on a bench in the summer park.
Trees are less green than the drum like a long gourd
one pounds with the heels of his palms.

                                                   The other
has twin small drums his fingers tap like a lover's
fondling
            a girl's hard little breasts.
Slow, the long
                drum
                      booms;
the twin drums flutter and snap. Rhythms
hot as an orange shirt
                   open
                          on cocoa-colored skin,
rhythms
            bold as a vermilion shirt
under a black face blind with consummation.
Brilliance mates with brilliance
                    to assert
wealth as of tropical suns. The colors drum
like the heartbeats of boys flooded with salt joy,
with health shouting like Nile and Niger and Zambezi in
    tumult and unison.
It strikes the streets dumb,
                        the dusty park
hears only the speech of two shirts
on two dark drumming boys. Orange. Vermilion.

ANOTHER AUTUMN

A flotilla of clouds by its flocculence lightly defines
That purity of azure. Clouds by Tiepolo.
Earth, beneath, by Midas. Whose shining pleasure
Is in gold only, sometimes in a parent of gold or in
    golden siblings.
His huge orb, roseate gold, was lately a maple
In a green summer. These mulberry satin weaves,
Tinged with a lesser flagrance, were simple leaves where
Dogwood's ivory sprang; they chime like crystals
Of a parcel-gilt chandelier, in a hall rich with crimsons.
That oak in August spoke giant words, but was never as now
Sovereign, never so roundly sounded
Such resonance of bronze: a gold sombred,
Tuned to the chord of autumn. It will pass,
Is passing. Yet in this cool November light
The vibrance lives, lives as if it could never cease to
    hold
The wonder, as if it would both spend and keep
The essential gold, tell over and over the glory
That cannot be told.

TIVOLI : COPENHAGEN

To the memory of the indomitable "Lioness",
the BARONESS KAREN BLIXEN

The Chinese lanterns are hanging like fiery fruit
Beyond the gate invisibly engraved:
"Abandon despair, you who enter here."
They star the blossomy paths to the pagoda
That a Chinese emperor gave to a Danish king.
Here's everything that royalty or childhood could desire.
It is Hans Christian's world, without his sorrow.
Until tomorrow, all the toys are alive. The brave tin
    soldier
Comes marching along with his full company
To martial music that Mars never heard of,
Till the heart beats beats, beats beats like a thaumaturgic
Drum. The pagoda floats on a lake.
Ducks and a swan and giant dragonflies that are
    winged lanterns
Or mosquito traps float on a lake.
Another lake is for boating.
And another music blows in a gay gust
From another part of the forest:
Beethoven's Seventh, with a Chinese conducting.
The forest is rich with witches
And ghosts, and with Titania's people.

There are forest pools, of course, and, in the open,
    fountains
Where flames or bubbles of silver climb crystal columns.
Farther, screams of delighted fear
Shrill, whirling with the
Ferris-wheel, or bump shatteringly and jump with
The rollercoaster.
But there is generous quiet where the crowd attends

The mountebanks and acrobats, or, better:
The antics of Harlequin and the clown, applauding when
The stern father, the ingénue, and her lover
Give the pantomime a happy ending.
But the children shriek for the actors to speak,
If once only, to speak—those master mimes.
Who roar in answer, roar as the curtains close.

It is not night that descends, but dawn that rises
On this pleasure park for children and lovers,
And for those few ancients fallen in love with joy.
It is a love affair of the centuries, with always fresh
Delights in old surprises, with the strangeness of
The familiar marvels,
Where all creatures, as in the first Garden, are at home,
Where everything may enter, save despair.

IN HONOR OF HER SEVENTY-FIFTH BIRTHDAY

(November 12, 1962)

to

Mischievous moralist, we give you joy,
Admiring the years of your employ
Rewarded by the visits of a Muse
Inhabiting museums, wilds, and zoos.
An heiress of that vigilant recluse who
Never had seen a moor yet vowed she knew
No less just how the heather looks, you find
Exciting most, excursions of the mind.

Courage is needed for such escapades,
Revived when all assumed provision fades,
And courage is your maxim, burnished by
Irradiant piercing singularity.
Gracious to all but fools, you let us eye

Mouse at Versailles, roc, bison, crow, kiwi,
Ostrich and elephant; we thank you for
Over a dozen curious creatures more,
Robust yet delicate—so your poems entrance,
Enhancing virtue with wit's elegance.

A DAY IN LATE AUGUST

Depth on fathomless depth of blue, swept clean
Of all but two, perhaps three, cherubic clouds,
The sky is big and festive, like poetry.
Willow, dogwood, oak, elm, tulip tree,
Blue spruce, black walnut, match and march their greens
As in a procession stilled, on the still air.
Hilarity quivers within the grave scene
Like hidden life beneath water.
The air has the sweetness of grass, the grass
Sparkles freshly like air.
Alien or absent, every evil thing.
The most serene month in all the twelve
Summons "the daughter of laughter": a smile, to greet
The autumn that is coming, that is near.

VII

LIGHT VERSE, OCCASIONAL POEMS, JUVENILIA

BIRTHDAY SONG FOR
ALISON (ALISOUN) MUMFORD

From ear to ear rejoicings run
To hear the news of Alisoun.
Forever sweet be the renown—
Or old or young—of Alison!
The merriest bells chime in her name,
By any spelling 'tis the same:
A sound, a round, a carol of fun
Lapped in the syllables: Alisoun;
A boon, a tune, a rune to crown
Magic with melody: Alison.
Her mother's name is wisdom's own,
Her dad's means iron's way with stone;
Thus light and power have joined as one
To make most excellent Alisoun.
And let her brother's famous name
Add stature to her early fame,
And all proclaim in unison
Our blessings upon Alison!

September, 1935

ON THE AVENUE

Like the light on festive water
Streamlined motors flow and glitter;
Crisp as snow, the cellophane
Flaunts its wingspread like a fan.
Now for furred and perfumed ladies
Jewels leap from velvet shadows,
And for merry gentlemen
Flowers resign their haughty stems.
Frosty balsam, feathered angels
Stiffly grace the golden mangers
In a plate-glass panoply
Colder than the silver sky.
Time grows limp as Dali's watches
In the hurrying pilgrims' clutches
As the news from Asia roars
Wasplike in their urban ears.
Still the lustrous windows blazon
Forth the greetings of the season,
And held out to all who pass
Are the shops' good will and peace,
While the motors flow and glitter
Like the light on festive water.

December, 1941

THE TEACHERS*

The first academy was not the grove
Where Plato walked, to exercise his tongue,
And aired an old man's doubts about the young,
Like that boy, Aristotle (who later throve).

The first academy was nobler even
Than Athens', the paths there were pleasanter,
The trees grand, where a mere whisper made a stir.
Heaven knows, as the phrase goes, the place was heaven.

And the sole teacher was the cool, the nice,
The unremorseful serpent. It was he,
The Book says, founded our society:
The educator educed by Paradise.

His gloss was one that even a she could grapple.
Ethics, he knew this well, you never teach.
He simply slyly put it within reach,
As a shy child presents teacher an apple.

Who now recalls its savor, the fruit that gave
Knowledge of good and evil? None, any more.
Although, the tale tells, Eve reserved the core
For her offspring, having nothing else to save.

Her forethought in preserving it seemed plain,
So far from the banquet hall of the Waldorf Astoria.
Wanting her young to taste her own euphoria.
(Though how did she split that bit between Abel and Cain?)

* An occasional poem, composed for the 75th anniversary of the author's
school and slightly revised for inclusion here.

[179]

Ambivalent, those gifts the fruit afforded:
It meant being involved, meant parenthood
And pain, meant work, meant wars, the cross-grained good,
The smooth evil, with which actions are rewarded.

Say the first act was love, there is no disguising
The next was murder. A further fact is clear:
We've learned by doing. Where do we go from here?
Out there some planet should be worth colonizing.

Still, there's this nearest planet we can't blink:
This earth, divided like ourselves, that we
May learn how to compose, imperfectly.
We may yet learn thinking, if we try to think.

So, not too long ago, John Dewey taught,
If aught is ever taught, which is a question
For the genial hours devoted to digestion,
A word connoting processes of thought.

For all that, the rich vestiture of reason
Can turn to rags, as faded, squamous, damp,
As hang on the inmates of a prison camp,
Cursed in the frigid or the torrid season.

We've had famous reasoners: Aristotle, Plato,
Descartes, the gentle Darwin, Marx, and Freud,
Einstein. But when the heart is unemployed,
Their learning is not worth a cold potato.

And who can teach the heart? We are our own
Instructors, each beginning, a little late,
With little help, to explore his real estate,
Stumbling, undignified, in the half dark, alone.

We learn, perhaps, how much we just pretended
To understand, how deaf we were, how blind,
And a chief end of our learning is to find
The bounds of our ignorance have been extended.

Then let us not praise famous men, but praise
Imagination, experience: the two
Who instruct each other, as we rarely do;
Their bitter fruit gives fragrance to all our days.

Now, tasting it, we recognize the features
Of the few who pointed out that multiple fruit,
Who serpentwise helped us reach it. These we salute.
Are there, then, teachers?

e. e. cummingsesq*

: dearmrcummings it is
late
r than you th
ink ;printersink s
                print
ingdownand sp   (o)
                ill
    ing(
        ver)
            the
                page doesnt
excite or delight us
the same way anymore ;not
that we ask you to
stop (look Listen)
drinking
at the pierian sp
                ring(aroundarosie)
;but you must be
careful or you will get
all
!wet
we also admire
win-
    tree trunk leaf sky & sn
o wfl
akes ;prettygirls littlechildr
en-
during moons sl
O wtwi
lights flowers & loves brief

---

*These lines were published in 1941 as a review of Cummings' *50 POEMS*. They refer to the contents of that book only.

mercies
;and we like your
impudent balla
dry
;but
it is
nineteenfortyone mrcummings
,and you must forgive us
if we sometimes
y
  aaaw
     n
;because it is
appallingly
late.
hell is a thirsty place
and only
a draught from the top of
helicon will do ;we are not asking you for
something new ,simply
few
and (er
)orbetter
?poems

REFLECTIONS IN A LITTLE PARK

On dusty benches in the park
I see them sit from noon till dark,
Infirm and dull, or glum and dry,
And think, as I go stepping by:
"There—but for the grace of God—sit I!"
Yet cannot blink and cannot bless
God's manifest ungraciousness.

GREETINGS OF THE SEASON*

Here's English of the O.E.D.
And tongues of prouder pedigree;
Here's French, Italian, German, Latin,
Oh, an' the Scottish nae forgettin',
And Hebrew, eke, the language that
Was spoke before a sole "begat":
In Eden, before Eve affected
The ways that left her mate dejected.
Thanks for your Christmas stocking! it's
Knubbly with games to try our wits,
And sprinkled with bright salt of malice,
'Spite of the girl demure as Alice
Upon the cover of your greeting:
You offer savory and sweeting.
We smile at everything you send;
We smile, too, at the very end
When, casual, canny cavalier,
You bid us come "another year"
To visit you on the fine acres
You got from Talcotts and from Bakers.
That invitation makes us ponder.
And also we're inclined to wonder

* These lines, from the original in the Yale Collection of American Literature, were composed in response to a booklet entitled *Wilson's Christmas Stocking, Fun for Young and Old*, received by Edmund Wilson's friends at Christmas, 1953. The "Stocking"—though small, too bulky to reproduce here—contained "Scurrilous Clerihews, Anagrams on Eminent Authors, Easy Exercises in the Use of Difficult Words" and other goodies, including limericks of sorts, among them, in a mixture of English and Hebrew, "Something for my Jewish Friends" (this was printed on page 18). The word in Hebrew in my response is pronounced "ta-ahm" in English and means "taste". The spelling of Stillson was corrected in "A Christmas Stocking" as it appears in *Night Thoughts* by Edmund Wilson.

Why such a sage as Edmund Wilson
Gave but one meagre "l" to Stillson.
No matter! Here's a Christmas stocking
To keep brains racked and bodies rocking.
Accept best thanks, then, from Avrahm,
Who finds therein a lot of טעם.
Though page 18 eludes her yet,
Here, too, good wishes from

Babette.

December, 1953

A CAROL OUT OF SEASON

Now Christmas is over,
Beards, baubles, and bells
That made of Manhattan
A great Book of Kells
Are promptly forgotten,
Save this chief of sights:
The Library lions
In leis of lights.

In orchards of asphalt
Rich fruits were ablaze
That rapidly suffered
The blight of displays.
Yet remembrance will cherish,
Whatever it slights,
The Library lions
In leis of lights.

Come spring and come summer,
Come autumn, who thinks
Of bediamonded angels,
Madonnas in minks?
Still, in season or out,
One quaint vision invites:
The Library lions
In leis of lights.

January, 1956

ON FIRST EATING DOLPHIN

Plump as a cherub, black
As a black poodle's nose,
You flew as water flows—
Laughter upon your track.

Flying to dive, to leap
In a loop-the-loop of the sea:
Warm blood in rivalry
With the towering dance of the deep.

Dolphin, I've watched your play
Beyond the ship: you shone
Thunderbright, and were gone
Under fantastic spray.

Half legend and half beast;
Doomed by a sold-out god
To wear a shape so odd;
Or not among the least

Of the whale's cousins? And
Anciently emblem of
Diligence, speed, love,
What wonder you command!

Droll to behold, yet drolly
Graceful, well praised in song,
Good dolphin, you belong
To things the wise count holy.

And shall you be our meat,
With sauce, with rice, and wine?
Comical or divine
Or both, how can we eat

Your flesh? The wine's decanted;
We're served. Scared, curious,
We taste (why so much fuss?)
DOLPHIN. We ARE enchanted!

Belated Postscript

Here is a pretty pass!
On a false premise based,
Those words should be erased;
They hold no truth, alas!

The dolphin we presumed
A rich, cetaceous dish
Was no more than a fish.
It was in vain we plumed

Ourselves upon partaking
Of mythic fare. What matter—
No after-thought can spatter
The feast we then were making.

DOUBLE DACTYL

Fiddlety diddlety
Hecht atque Hollander,
Didacts and wits with a
Soupçon of Sade,

Made of the form that the
Former invented an
UltraDraconian
Joke on the *fade*.

"I KNEW"

I knew that the sky was blue,
And I knew that the sun was gold,
But I never knew that the earth was round
Until I was told.

March 13, 1901

"THERE I SAT"

There I sat in the lonely parlor
  With my little book in my hand;
It was such a lonely day in Winter,
  Not a bird sang around the land.
It made my heart feel sadder
  When I saw a fairy sit in my hand.

December, 1902

VIII

TRANSLATIONS

THE SOUL

Go thou
Her changing roads.
Know all her provinces.
Yet to her far frontiers thou shalt
Not come.

AFTER HERACLITUS

TANKA

Since he is too young
To know the way, I would plead:
"Pray, accept this gift,
O Underworld messenger,
And bear the child pick-a-back."

FROM THE JAPANESE OF OKURA

HAIKU

The falling flower
I saw drift back to the branch
Was a butterfly.

FROM THE JAPANESE OF MORITAKE

QUATRAIN

that Villon made when he was condemned to die

I'm François, I'm sorry to say,
Born in Paris, near Pontoise city.
Thanks to a rope six feet and a bitty
My neck will learn what my buttocks weigh.

FROM THE FRENCH OF FRANÇOIS VILLON

CORRESPONDENCES

Nature, a temple, has live pillars who
At whiles allow confused words issuance;
Man encounters many an intimate glance
From the forest of symbols that he passes through.

In a profound, shadowy unison,
Like lingering echoes distance has confounded,
As vast as night, like clarity unbounded,
Perfumes, colors, sounds, respond as one.

There are perfumes fresh as infants' flesh,
Dulcet as oboes, and like prairies, green,
—And others, rotten, richly triumphing,

Able to grow immense as infinite things,
Like amber, musk, benzoin, and frankincense,
Sing the transports of spirit and of sense.

FROM THE FRENCH OF CHARLES BAUDELAIRE

JOHN THE RIVER

River without a Land, ohé, John Landless' course,
The waters do not choose between the banks but flow
Onward between those rivals mutually bound
East-West, the Yes-and-No, the youthful and the slow.

Does he adjudicate between the hush, the cries?
He who knows well the springs' gestation underground,
Asks of the winds a vote of confidence, will trace
The figure of the flight on which the birds are bound.

Rightward he views the aging walls of Nineveh,
And ancient kings who fling their rubies to the base
And sees the powerful palace betray itself at last
And the descending rain displume proud Samothrace.

Upon the other shore he sees the Amazons
Plunge freely where the cunning billow braves,
Their large frank eyes, enriched with belladonna, keen
To pierce the ancient secret of the incestuous waves.

Fishers and riverfolk will stand before their huts
To watch the river flow, not jealous of his glory,
Let him seek out the spirit in regions far from here
If they may fish and drink and beach a loaded dory.

River without a Land, its wave ephemeral,
Down to the sea it flows, no choice, no faltering
Between peace on the right and war upon the left
From dawn quick with desire to dusk remembering.

FROM THE FRENCH OF YVAN GOLL

LANDLESS JOHN SALUTES
THE HARLEM RIVER

This water this black alcohol that draws us on
This white whiskey where black eyes are swimming
These sulphurous pools where black flies are flowering
These green dragons and black dragons of the plague

O sorrowful wave
White dance   black dance   red dance   yellow dance
Dance of all the seas that give suck as one breast
Massacre of all mothers that choke as one throat

      Harlem! Black priestess
      Drunk on the white milk of the dew

O river with mole-colored hair
And a scintillant girdle of salmon russet steel
Chaldean dancer in this dirty hole of America
Pinning a moon of gold between your filthy breasts
Toward you descend the cats of our flesh
And the reflections of our shattered sheet-iron

O ancient wave
Wave of the yellow Tigris and of pitchy Harlem
My pillow is stuffed with the scales of cheap fish
Sad wave overwhelmed
By so many drowned heads
Somber river which defies the ocean
With its sluices of death

FROM THE FRENCH OF YVAN GOLL

"COME TO THE PARK"

Come to the park now left for dead and see ;
The shimmer of far shores whose smile is cool •
The startling blue of clouds whose clarity
Brightens the motley paths and every pool •

Take the deep yellow • and the velvet grey
Of birch and box • this wind remembers May •
The tardy roses not quite withered drip
Fragrance • then pluck and touch petalled lip •

Nor pass these final asters' radiance •
The purple caught in tendrils of wild vine
And what remains of green life intertwine
Lightly above the autumnal countenance •

FROM THE GERMAN OF STEFAN GEORGE

SPANISH DANCER

As in the hand a sulphur-match burns white
before it flames, and giddily unfurls
its quivering tongues:—so, circling in the sight
of crowding watchers, hurried hot and bright
her rounded dance quivers in widening swirls.

And suddenly it is sheer flame aflare.

Tossing a glance the girl kindles her hair
and with more daring art whirls her attire
wholly, at once, into this furious fire,
from which her bare arms, each a startled snake,
stretch sinuously, rattling as they wake.

And then: as if the fire were strangling stuff
she gathers it together—flings it off
imperiously, with a prouder mien, her eyes
watch: there upon the ground, raging, it lies
and keeps on flaming and will not give place.—
Yet certain of her triumph, with a sweet
welcome now in her smile, she lifts her face
and stamps it out with little resolute feet.

FROM THE GERMAN OF RAINER MARIA RILKE

"IN ALL THESE THINGS"

In all these things I cherish as a brother
still it is you I find; seedlike you wait,
basking serenely in the narrowest compass,
and greatly give yourself in what is great.

This is the marvel of the play of forces,
that they so serve the things wherethrough they flow;
growing in roots, to dwindle in the tree-trunks,
and in the crowns like resurrection show.

FROM THE GERMAN OF RAINER MARIA RILKE

"PUT OUT MY EYES"

Put out my eyes, and I can see you still;
slam my ears to, and I can hear you yet;
and without any feet can go to you;
and tongueless I can conjure you at will.
Break off my arms, I shall take hold of you
and grasp you with my heart as with a hand;
arrest my heart, my brain will beat as true;
and if you set this brain of mine afire,
then on my blood I yet will carry you.

FROM THE GERMAN OF RAINER MARIA RILKE

"ALTHOUGH, AS FROM A PRISON"

Although, as from a prison walled with hate,
each from his own self labors to be free,
the world yet holds a wonder, and how great!
ALL LIFE IS LIVED: now this comes home to me.
But who, then, lives it? Things that patiently
stand there, like some unfingered melody
that sleeps within a harp as day is going?
Is it the winds, across the waters blowing?
Is it the branches, beckoning each to each,
is it the flowers, weaving fragrances,
the aging alleys that reach out endlessly?
Is it the warm beasts, moving to and fro,
or the birds, alien as they sail from view?
This life—who lives it really? God,—do you?

FROM THE GERMAN OF RAINER MARIA RILKE

"YOU ARE THE FUTURE"

You are the future, the great sunrise red
above the broad plains of eternity.
You are the cock-crow when time's night was fled,
you are the dew, the matins, and the maid,
the stranger and the mother, you are death.

You are the changeful shape that out of Fate
rears up in everlasting solitude,
the unlamented and the unacclaimed,
beyond describing as some savage wood.

You are the deep epitome of things
that keeps its being's secret with locked lip,
and shows itself to others otherwise:
to the ship, a haven—to the land, a ship.

FROM THE GERMAN OF RAINER MARIA RILKE

MORGUE

LITTLE ASTER

A drowned truck-driver was propped on the slab.
Someone had stuck a lavender aster
between his teeth.
As I cut out the tongue and the palate,
through the chest
under the skin
with my long knife,
I must have touched the flower, for it slid
into the brain lying next.
I packed it into the cavity of the chest
among the excelsior
as it was sewn up.
Drink yourself full in your vase!
Rest softly,
little aster.

FROM THE GERMAN OF GOTTFRIED BENN

MORGUE

LOVELY CHILDHOOD

The mouth of a girl who had long lain among the reeds
    looked gnawed away.
As the breast was cut open, the gullet showed
    full of holes.
Finally in a cavity below the diaphragm
a nest of young rats was discovered.
One little sister lay dead.
The others thrived on liver and kidneys,
drank the cold blood and
enjoyed a lovely childhood there.
And sweet and swift came their death also:
They were all thrown into the water together.
Oh, how the little muzzles squeaked!

FROM THE GERMAN OF GOTTFRIED BENN

PAUSE IN THE FIRING

Perhaps there is an inkling of the order to come
Perhaps mischief already runs in your veins
All Bethlehem's towers are striking ten
Come sister let us push on toward the miracle

Make yourself neat be friendly and easy
The pack of fears I take on my back
I a veteran tired but no coward
Come dear sister stay close beside me

We share the night and the abandoned house
But first we must bury clock and key
Now while the guns of time remain silent
Hunched in the trench we push on toward the miracle

Do not look up to stare after the flares
I will tear the barbed wire for you with my hands
I know all the secret trails through the minefields
There is only one star that leads us on

Do not cry sister leave your shoes in the mud
Soon the guns will resume then we must be there
On all the towers squats the mischief to come
Give me your hand we must push on toward the miracle

FROM THE GERMAN OF WALTER NEUMANN

GRAPES

I shall not miss the roses, fading
When springtime's hurrying days are done;
I love the grapes whose clusters ripen
Upon the hillsides in the sun—
The glory of my fertile valley,
They hang, each lustrous as a pearl,
Gold autumn's joy, oblong, transparent,
Like the slim fingers of a girl.

FROM THE RUSSIAN OF ALEXANDER PUSHKIN

"HERE'S WINTER"

Here's winter. Far from town, what shall we do? I question
The servant bringing in my morning cup of tea:
"How is the weather—warm? Not storming? The ground's
    covered
With freshly fallen snow?" Come, is it best to be
Astride a horse at once, or shall we, until dinner,
See what our neighbor's old reviews may have to say?
The snow is fresh and fine. We rise and mount our horses,
And trot through fields agleam with the first light of day.
We carry whips; the dogs run close behind our stirrups;
With careful eyes we search the snow, we scour the plain
For tracks, ride round and round, and tardily at twilight,
After we've missed two hares, at last turn home again.
How jolly! Evening comes: without, a storm is howling;
The candlelight is dim. The heart is wrenched with pain.
Slow drop by drop I drink my boredom's bitter poison.
I try a book. The eyes glide down the page—in vain:
My thoughts are far away . . . and so I close the volume,
Sit down, take up my pen, force my dull Muse to say
Some incoherent words, but melody is wanting,
The sounds won't chime. . . . The devil! Where now
    is the way
I had with rhyme? I can't control this curious handmaid:
The verse is shapeless, cold, so lame it cannot walk.
So I dismiss the Muse: I am too tired to quarrel.
I step into the parlor where I hear them talk

About the sugar-works, about the next election;
The hostess, like the weather, frowns, her only arts
Are plying rapidly her long steel knitting needles
And telling people's fortunes by the king of hearts.
How dismal! Thus the days go by, alike and lonely.
But if, while I play draughts at twilight in my nook,
Into our dreary village a closed sleigh or carriage
Should just by chance bring guests for whom I did not look:
Say, an old woman and two girls, her two young daughters
(Tall, fair-haired creatures, both), the place that was so
    dull,
So Godforsaken, all at once is bright and lively,
And suddenly, good heavens, life grows rich and full!
Attentive sidelong looks, and then a few words follow,
There's talk, then friendly laughter, and songs when
    lamps are lit,
And after giddy waltzes there are languid glances,
There's whispering at table, gay and ready wit;
Upon the narrow stairs a lingering encounter;
When twilight falls, a girl steals from her wonted place
And out onto the porch, bare-throated, chest uncovered—
The wind is up, the snow blows straight into her face!
Unhurt by northern blasts the Russian rose will blow.
How hotly a kiss burns in keen, frosty weather!
How fresh a Russian girl blooming in gusts of snow!

FROM THE RUSSIAN OF ALEXANDER PUSHKIN

MY COUNTRY

I love my country, but that love is odd:
My reason has no part in it at all!
Neither her glory, bought with blood,
Nor her proud strength hold me in thrall;
No venerable customs stir in me
The pleasant play of reverie.
Ask me not why I love, but love I must
Her fields' cold silences,
Her somber forests swaying in a gust,
Her rivers at the flood like seas.
I love to rattle on rough roads at night,
My lodging still to find, while half awake
I peer through shadows left and right
And watch the lights of mournful hamlets quake.
I love the smoke above singed stubble rising;
I love a caravan that winds forlorn
Across the steppe; I love surprising
Two birches white above the yellow corn.
A well-stocked barn, a hut with a thatched roof,
Carved shutters on a village window: these
Are simple things in truth,
But few can see them as my fond eye sees.
And on a holiday, from dewy dusk until
Midnight, it is a boon for me
To watch the dancers stomping to the shrill
Loud babble of the drunken peasantry.

FROM THE RUSSIAN OF MIKHAIL LERMONTOV

START OF LONG-RANGE BOMBING

Abruptly all was changed: the hurrying crowd
Could not accommodate its daily round
To what it heard, knew only that it heard
Neither a city nor a country sound.
True, it was like a brother to the roll
Of distant thunder, but the thunder spends
The moisture and the freshness of high clouds,
Its mutterings are promises—a friend's.
It brings the rumor of the gaiety
Of showers that the fields are avid for;
But this noise was an arid one: it scorched;
The anguished ear could not believe the roar
Would mount, would swell, would spread
Until my child was numbered with the dead.

FROM THE RUSSIAN OF ANNA AKHMATOVA

EPILOGUE TO *REQUIEM*

I learned how faces that were fresh grow gaunt,
How dread peers out from under half-shut lids,
How suffering covers cheeks with line on line
Of cuneiform's rough arrowheads and grids;

How hair, ash blond or black, suddenly turns
Grey; how on obedient lips a smile but half
Formed fades away, and witheringly
Fear quivers in a little arid laugh;

And I pray, not for myself alone,
But for everyone who stood with me, all, all
Who stood in the bitter cold, in the July heat,
Beneath the red, blinded wall.

FROM THE RUSSIAN OF ANNA AKHMATOVA

FROM THE ORIENTAL NOTEBOOK

How drunk we were, each with the other, that
    marvellous night,
when only the Asian darkness gave us light,
and the irrigation canals were murmuring
and the black carnations' scent pierced like a sting.

And we walked alone through a city not ours, through
    a savage song
and midnight heat—the Serpent coiled among
the constellations in the thick-starred skies,
and we did not dare to turn and meet one another's eyes.

And it seemed as if ages walked with us, unseen,
and as if an invisible hand were striking a tambourine,
and there were stranger sounds, like something we must
    mark:
secret signals that whirled about us there in the dark.

Thus once, and only once, we walked together, as though
we had got into no human story, and, of a sudden, the glow
of the moon like a diamond sailboat swam into view
over our parting meeting, the single encounter we knew.

And should that night return to you also, mind
my wish, however belated, oh, be kind
and send me, waking or dreaming, by my choice
this: an Asian reed pipe's slender voice.

FROM THE RUSSIAN OF ANNA AKHMATOVA

THE URALS FOR THE FIRST TIME

Without an accoucheuse, in darkness, pushing her
Blind hands against the night, the Ural fastness, torn and
Half-dead with agony, was screaming in a blur
Of mindless pain, as she was giving birth to morning.

And brushed by chance, tall ranges far and wide
Loosed toppling bronze pell-mell in thunder-colored
    rumbling.
The train panted and coughed, clutching the mountainside,
And at that sound the ghosts of fir trees shied and
    stumbled.

The smoky dawn was a narcotic for the peaks,
A drug with which the fire-breathing dragon plied them,
As when a specious thief upon a journey seeks
To lull his fellow travelers with opium slipped them slyly.

They woke on fire. The skies were poppy-colored flame,
Whence Asiatics skied like hunters after quarry;
To kiss the forests' feet the eager strangers came
And thrust upon the firs the regal crowns they carried.

Arrayed in majesty, in ranks the firs arose,
Those shaggy dynasts, their grave glory clamant,
And trod the orange velvet of the frozen snows
Spread on a tinseled cloth and richly damasked.

FROM THE RUSSIAN OF BORIS PASTERNAK

THREE VARIATIONS

1

When consummate the day hangs before you,
Each detail to be scanned at your ease,
Just the sultry chatter of squirrels
Resounds in the resinous trees.

And storing up strength in their languor,
The ranked piney heights are adrowse,
While the freckled sweat is pouring
From the peeling forest's boughs.

2

Miles thick with torpor nauseate the gardens.
The catalepsy of the valleys' rage
Is weightier, more threatening than a tempest,
Fiercer than hurricane's most savage raid.

The storm is near. The dry mouth of the garden
Gives off the smell of nettles, roofs, and fear,
And of corruption; and the cattle's bellow
Rises columnar in the static air.

3

Now tatters of denuded clouds
Grow on each bush in tasseled groves.
Damp nettles fill the garden's mouth.
It smells of storms and treasure troves.

The shrubs are tired of lament.
In heaven arched prospects multiply.
Like web-toed birds on swampy ground
The barefoot azure treads the sky.

And willow branches and the leaves
Of oaks, and tracks beside the spring,
Like lips the hand has not wiped dry,
Are glistening, are glistening.

FROM THE RUSSIAN OF BORIS PASTERNAK

"IF ONLY, WHEN I MADE MY DEBUT"

If only, when I made my debut,
There might have been a way to tell
That lines with blood in them can murder,
That they can flood the throat and kill,

I certainly would have rejected
A jest on such a sour note,
So bashful was that early interest,
The start was something so remote.

But age is pagan Rome, demanding
No balderdash, no measured breath,
No fine feigned parody of dying,
But really being done to death.

A line that feeling sternly dictates
Sends on the stage a slave, and, faith,
It is good-bye to art forever
Then, then things smack of soil and Fate.

FROM THE RUSSIAN OF BORIS PASTERNAK

MARCH

Blazing sun that fairly makes you swelter,
Crazed, the whole ravine is rampaging.
Like the labors of a sturdy milkmaid,
Spring's incessant chores are in full swing.

Snow is wasting, feeble with anemia,
Branchlets of blue veins betray decline.
But the cow barn seethes: there life is smoking,
Health glows radiant on the pitchforks' tines.

Oh, these days, these days and nights! At midday,
Drops are drumming, while the driblets spill
From the eaves where icicles are failing;
Chatter of those never-ceasing rills!

Flung wide open—stable, shed, and cow barn.
Pigeons peck oats from the snow, and there:
Giver of life, answerable for all this—
Dung, fresh fallen, smells of the fresh air.

FROM THE RUSSIAN OF BORIS PASTERNAK

"FOR THE SAKE OF THE THUNDROUS VALOR"

For the sake of the thundrous valor of coming ages,
And the towering tribe of man, I paid the cost,
Forfeited more than my place at the feast of my fathers,
Too, my gaiety fled, my repute was lost.

Horribly, a wolfhound leapt on my shoulders,
But the blood of a wolf does not run in my veins,
Rather tuck me away, like a cap in the sleeve of
A heavy greatcoat fit for Siberia's plains.

Then I'll not see the squelching filth nor the cowards,
Nor on the wheel the bloodied bones of the strong,
Broken; instead, in their primal beauty,
The blue foxes will shine for me all night long.

Lead me into the dark where the Yenisei rushes,
Where, grazing the dawn, the fir trees rear,
For the blood of a wolf does not run in my body,
And none shall kill me who is not my peer.

FROM THE RUSSIAN OF OSIP MANDELSHTAM

"HOURS OF SLEEPLESSNESS"

Hours of sleeplessness. Homer. Taut sails. Tonight
I've read half through the catalogue of ships, that
   spreading
Clamorous brood which rose up over Hellas, heading
For Troy, those ships that are a troop of cranes in
   flight—

A wedge of cranes that flies toward lands hidden from view.
Divine the foam asperging the heads of kings. Ah, tell us
Where do you sail, Achæans? What takes you forth
   from Hellas?
Were it not for Helen, what would Troy be to you?

The sea, and Homer—all is moved by love. I wonder,
Which should I listen to? Homer is hushed. The roar
Of the black sea goes gnashing on, a furious orator,
And near my pillow now looses its ponderous thunder.

FROM THE RUSSIAN OF OSIP MANDELSHTAM

I am to the present-day tribe
just a long dirty joke, but I
see him crossing the mountains of time,
him whom nobody sees.

Where bobtailed eyes fall short—
at the head of hungry hordes,
revolutions his crown of thorns,
the year 'Sixteen draweth nigh.

And I
prepare the way.
Wherever there's pain I am there;
and where tears rain,
on every drop I crucify
myself.
It's too late now to forgive.
I've scorched the souls
where tenderness could live,
and that's a tougher job than capturing
a thousand thousand Bastilles.

And when,
announcing its arrival
by revolt,
you go to meet the savior,
I will bolt
ahead, drag out my soul for you,
trample it,
flatten it to a big rag!
and give it to you,
bleeding, for your flag.

FROM THE RUSSIAN OF VLADIMIR MAYAKOVSKY

OVIDIOPOLIS

Yes, Ovid,
I had a view of it:
Your little Ovidiopolis.
It was quiet, except for the wind banging the wickets;
Hard to say which was more trying, the quiet, or the wind,
Flying from the Euxine over the Dniester estuary.
I know, Ovid,
It was not very merry
Sitting at those smoky fires with the Getae in sheepskins,
You so badly wanting to talk,
Balked by their uncouth language.

Talk about what?
The Parrhasian Virgin, Callisto.
She twined her icy breath with what little heat remained
Under this moon, that waxes and wanes
Above a land that for you was the bleak end of the world.
For us, seeing that winters here, if sharp, are short,
This is the South, the gate beyond which an eternal
     summer waits.
But more than half converted to your view,
I gave a bitter laugh,
And echoed your lament:
"Here, alone and lonely, cast on the shores of the
     seven-mouthed Dniester,
I have come under the spell of the Parrhasian Virgin. . . ."

Perhaps we can toy with the name
And lay claim to it as Par-Russian?
Perhaps she'd a bit of the look of those Russian virgins
    to come,
One of the sisters now traipsing along the estuary,
Snaring the songs of the world on their pocket transistors,
Hanging about the ferry,
Trying to catch a taxi to Odessa. And this Odessa screams
As noisily as the city of your dreams, your Rome.

But you, crouched at your fire with the ancient Getae,
So homesick, you would just as soon be dead,
My poor old Ovid,
This never entered your head!

                FROM THE RUSSIAN OF LEONID MARTYNOV

THE FOREIGNER

In the seaport of Archangel,
foreign ships early and late,
foreign sorrow in that seaport,
foreign fate.

Like a rook, a young one, swarthy,
all the white night through, you lie
huddled beside Peter's statue,
small Greek seaman, and you cry.

Not in any foreign fashion,
on the dusty square you smear
drunkenly, with dirty knuckles,
that dark face of yours with tears.

Did the skipper bawl you out, boy?
Someone in your family die?
Maybe you've had too much vodka?
Nothing's right, you don't know why?

What on earth has happened to you?
Greek, where is it you were hit?
What has happened is quite simple:
You are human—and that's it.

There's a sailor from a schooner,
Russian; liquored up, he slumps,
lurching, copper-faced, no question
but the fellow's in the dumps.

Down he sits beside the Greek now:
"How about a drink, chum, eh?"
And into his leather jacket
his huge rough hand makes its way.

Deft and serious, from the pocket
pulls a pint-interpreter,
bangs the bottle's neck against the
bench; the Greek does not demur.

Arm in arm, the two together
sit in silence there and booze,
as into the farther distance
stare Greek grief and Russian blues.

FROM THE RUSSIAN OF YEVGENY YEVTUSHENKO

A FRAGMENT OF SKY

A fragment of sky melted onto the ice
Wind wiped it away
Wind gathered clouds   wind wiped them away
And wiped away the ice

                all but two gulls the shape of snow

FROM THE FINNISH OF TUOMAS ANHAVA

ORPHEUS 7

I play, there is no answer.
The sea darkens.
On the branch, bronze leaves
quiveringly stiffen.
Moon, stars, order themselves in silence,
there is no motion.
I wander,
firm frail instrument of marrow and bone.

Reversed,
the landscape.
To a hollow mirror
I play the expanse of space inverted,
for the sake of opposed harmonies,
slow narrowing music,
the vanishing, the not heard.

FROM THE FINNISH OF EEVA-LIISA MANNER

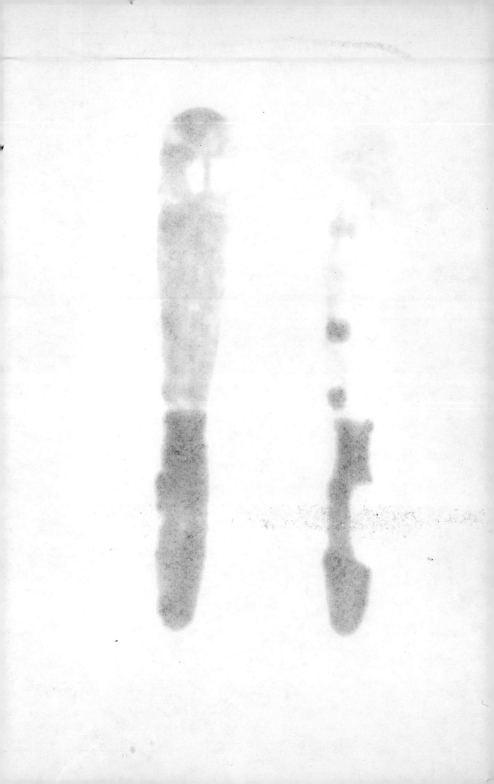